STEAM
TRACKED
BACK

STEAM
TRACKED
BACK

Trains in retrospect, 1967-60

**Richard Inwood
& Mike Smith**

SLP

First published in 2011

British Library Cataloguing in Publication Data

A catalogue record for this book is available from the British Library.

ISBN 978 1 85794 383 2

Silver Link Publishing Ltd
The Trundle
Ringstead Road
Great Addington
Kettering
Northants NN14 4BW

Tel/Fax: 01536 330588
email: sales@nostalgiacollection.com
Website: www.nostalgiacollection.com

Printed and bound in the Czech Republic

Front cover Steam tracked back: reference to maps and diaries failed at first to identify where exactly Richard took this photograph of a 'large Prairie' with an up freight south of Oxford in the early summer of 1965. Then a friend suggested that the signal box might be Sandford, and a recent visit confirmed the location. The box closed in December 1964, leaving no sign of any signalling just five or six months later. However, in 2011 the concrete fence-posts are still going strong! *RNI*

Half title Steam disappearing (1): an 'O2' 0-4-4 tank leaves Haven Street for Cowes on 3 April 1965. *MES*

Page 2 Steam disappearing (2): 'Black 5' No 45005 heads south towards Oxenholme with a freight on 26 August 1965. *MES*

Title page Steam receding: Richard seizes the moment to make the best of a bad job as the train taking him to Oxford for a 'bizarre ritual' (see the text) overtakes a GWR 'Hall' 4-6-0 somewhere north of the University city on a wintry 15 March 1964. *RNI*

Above Steam lingering on: the clouds in the damp Devon air come from an 'N' 2-6-0, acting as banker to Collett 'Mogul' No 6326 on the climb from Braunton to Mortehoe & Woolacombe with the 8.00am Wolverhampton-Ilfracombe on 15 August 1964. *RNI*

Back cover Steam retreating: first impressions suggest wrong-line working, but the direction of the steam confirms that 4F No 44247 is actually on a banking turn, at Peak Forest on 21 March 1964. This is the last in a sequence of shots, the rest of which are on page 21. *RNI*

CONTENTS

Foreword   7

Prologue: digging down, looking back   9

1 Frenzied pursuits: 'Up North', 1967-65   12
2 When you've got to go…: 'Down South', 1966-63   23
3 The right place at the right time: 'Out West', 1964   49
4 On the doorstep: the home patch, 1965-60   76
5 Sit back and wait: the WCML and the WRML, 1965-62   103
6 There for the taking: more cops for your money, 1963-61   118

Epilogue: those were the days   133
Acknowledgements   142
Abbreviations   142
Index of photographic locations   143

To Liz Inwood and Ruth Smith, with love and gratitude

Left This is Walton Well Road bridge, north of Oxford station and south of the junction with the Cambridge line. In several spans the bridge crosses the canal, the railway, and an offshoot of the canal, as seen in this image. Here it forms a frame for a 'Grange', which now cannot be identified – no smokebox plates, and a poorly painted number on the cab – on the 10.08 York-Bournemouth in summer 1965. *RNI*

Below left Richard and Liz met in Oxford, and Mike met Ruth in Cambridge. Forty-five years later, Liz (left) and Ruth stand on the former Oxford-Cambridge line of the LNWR where it crosses the River Ouse between Bedford and Willington. *RNI*

Opposite One of the models in Pete Waterman's wonderful collection is of Great Western 'Castle' No 5054 *Earl of Ducie*. On 9 May 1964 this engine (paired with a later style of tender) was used on the final stage of the famous Ian Allan 'Great Western' special from Paddington to the West of England and return, when four of the class had been fettled up in the hope of 100mph – which unfortunately was not quite achieved. It is seen here climbing towards West Bromwich on 18 July that year with the 9.40am Eastbourne-Wolverhampton. Since 9 May it has acquired a coat of grime, but also a coat of silver paint on the buffers. *MES*

FOREWORD
BY PETE WATERMAN

What makes you buy a book? More than likely it's because something catches your eye and your imagination in the promised content or on the front cover so you pick it up and you think 'This looks interesting!' and you happily spend your money.

When I was asked to do the Foreword for this book something rang a bell and I was reminded of a book that I had bought in 2009 called *Moved By Steam*, which was basically written around photographs that had been taken by people who were obviously steam nuts – like myself. I guessed they were about my age and they were definitely in the same mould, so I bought the book and read it with great interest as it really mirrored my own youth. I tend to like books that can give you a warm glow.

Now this book, *Steam Tracked Back*, gives me an even warmer glow. The period it focuses on is the time that I had begun working on the railways and had started to take for granted some of what the pictures show. This is the classic period! A time when one age was disappearing (that we never thought would) and another was just beginning, a new era. The photographs in this book are a true depiction of what I believe every enthusiast saw on the railway at that time. Not staged, not waiting for the right light, just showing a determination to capture the railway scene at the time. Most of the pictures relate to an area of the country that I knew only too well, and those illustrating the area around Leamington Spa bring back so many memories for me. If you aren't old enough to remember this period, then trust me, this was exactly what it looked like.

So here is another book for my shelf and one that will take me back to some very happy spotting days on my Hercules bike! I only wish I knew where all the friends were now who took those trips with me! I can tell you everything that happened to the locos, but sadly I can't remember what happened to those friends!

Oh, to get me Hercules bike back with its Sturmey Archer gears – the saddle might pinch a bit nowadays, though!

Above Steam disappearing (3): Kitson 'Dock Tank' 0-4-0ST No 47006 looks about to be entombed as it disappears under the road bridge on the Steeple Grange branch of the C&HPR on 16 July 1965. One can't help seeing this as a metaphor, not only for the imminent disappearance of the C&HPR, but also for that of steam on the whole BR system. *RNI*

Opposite The same location 45 years on. The Steeple Grange Light Railway now operates here and its narrow gauge track can just be glimpsed through the vegetation. *RNI*

Prologue: digging down, looking back

RICHARD: Ten years or so ago, Mike Smith and I, friends and fellow railway enthusiasts since our schooldays, realised that our collection of images featuring steam operation in the 1960s was quite a large one. That discovery resulted in our previous book for The Nostalgia Collection, *Moved by Steam: Beside the tracks and on the trains, 1962-67* (Silver Link Publishing, 2009). Delighted by its reception, we have been looking through the archive again, reliving those far-off days and seeking to raise the ghosts of steam once more for our own and for your enjoyment. This time we have also quarried more extensively from another deposit, containing printed matter such as tickets, timetables and magazines, and our own manuscript sources – notebooks, diaries, and logs of journeys behind steam.

We have dug down, like archaeologists, through all this material, exposing with each fresh stratum a different stage in our experience of steam, and a different aspect of it. Needless to say, the lower the layer, the older it is. So, whereas in *Moved by Steam* the reverser was in forward gear, here it is set to go backwards and the book proceeds in (roughly) reverse chronological order. Naturally, the time-line is not quite straight; as archaeologists and geologists know, layers can overlap, so just occasionally we have to turn the reverser the other way again to make sense of the story.

There is also a spatial dimension. Like most enthusiasts, we turned our attention to different parts of the system as the Modernisation Plan took hold; where steam survived, there we went. So the earlier chapters – later in time – deal with particular geographical areas. Earlier in time, steam was everywhere, and (money permitting) so were we; towards the end of the book, therefore, the focus is wider. For three areas, Burton-on-Trent, where we grew up, Oxford, where I spent my university days, and the Peak District, near to which my wife, Liz, and I intend to retire, we have included a number of 'past and present' shots, to show what has happened to the places that meant most to us.

The remainder of this chapter illustrates our method and suggests what we are seeking to achieve in the book as a whole. We will start bang up to date, then dig down through our material to the earliest level.

On 12 November 2010, after several fruitless visits and much consultation of maps by Mike and myself, I located the spot at which on 16 July 1965 I had photographed 'Dock Tank' No 47006 on the Steeple Grange branch of the Cromford & High Peak Railway. (Earlier that day I had managed to hitch a ride on its footplate.) The 'past' and 'present' shots appear opposite and below.

I have a particular nostalgic affection for

the C&HPR. In the last years of its life it was operated by two classes of saddle tank: Kitson's LMS 0-4-0 'Dock Tank' and the 'Austerity' 0-6-0, Riddles's wartime design for the Ministry of Supply. Seventy-five of the latter, built by Hunslet, were purchased after the war by the LNER, and passed into British Railways stock at nationalisation as Class 'J94'.

For my 60th birthday Liz treated me to a driving experience on Peak Rail's 'Austerity' 0-6-0ST, not one of the LNER/BR Hunslets but Robert Stephenson & Hawthorns' No 7136 of 1944, formerly WD150 *Royal Pioneer*. It is now in BR livery and numbered 68013 in memory of a former 'J94' denizen of the line. It took me a long while to cash in the voucher, but on 24 August 2010 I had a great time driving twice to Matlock and back from Darley Dale!

Further back still – just over a year in fact – from my earlier footplate experience on 47006, some friends and I had chased the RCTS excursion from Parsley Hay to Cromford. As documented in more detail in *Moved by Steam*, the passengers (or should they be called 'freight'…?) were hauled successively by a 'B1',

two 'J94s', a Kitson 'Dock Tank', and another 'J94', before being collected at Cromford by the same 'B1' as had delivered them to Parsley Hay.

Then, as I got down to the lowest levels of my collection, I discovered a Brownie 127 photograph of a 'J94' with a cement wagon. At first I was at a loss to recall its location. However, Mike's notebooks came to the rescue once more, and we found it had been captured on a visit to Bidston MPD (6F) on the "Wanderers" Railfans' Club excursion of 27 April 1962 (see also page 131).

Though, sadly, there is no photographic record, we discovered from a bizarre page in one of Mike's notebooks that we had seen the original 'J94', No 68013 (whose lookalike I drove), four years to the day before I photographed 47006: at Buxton MPD (9D) on the WRC excursion of 16 July 1961.

The journey on which we are about to take you tracks back, both as you move through the book and (as far as possible) down through each chapter too. Hence our title, *Steam Tracked Back: Trains in retrospect, 1967-60*.

Richard stands proudly by Peak Rail's 'Austerity' 0-6-0ST, now numbered 68013, at Darley Dale station after his driving experience on 24 August 2010. *Liz Inwood*

Above Here, on 27 June 1964, the paying passengers of the RCTS excursion – elegantly dressed for the occasion – are travelling towards Sheep Pasture from Middleton Bottom. The locomotive is our friend No 47006. *RNI*

Below 'J94' 0-6-0ST No 68066 shunts a cement wagon near Bidston MPD on 27 April 1962. *RNI*

Above Buxton shed was the last depot on the "Wanderers" Railfans' Club tour of 16 July 1961 (see the text). What a wonderful variety of locos, from 'J94' No 68013 (see opposite) to the 0-4-4 tanks formerly used on the Millers Dale branch! Nearly as remarkable is the 14-year-old Mike's assessment of the day, which shows what a grip the world of school had on his imagination, second only to that of trains. Sheds are ranked by number of cops, the percentage of cops is calculated in relation to the total of engines seen, the comment 'Very Good' appears in three different forms, and there is an apparently meaningless outburst of ticks, signatures and marks out of 10, these last imitating the handwriting of three members of the Burton Grammar School staff. What would an Educational Psychologist have made of it? *RNI*

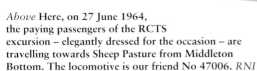

1
FRENZIED PURSUITS: 'UP NORTH', 1967-65

RICHARD: As everyone knows, the last rites of British steam were celebrated in North West England in 1968. By that time, our boyhood hobby had given way to other preoccupations: for me, the Christian faith and the prospect of a year in Uganda; for Mike, the natural world, especially plants; for both of us, academic study and the opposite sex. Some at least of these had begun to encroach some while before, so the topmost layer of our 'dig' contains less material than we'd like. Still, we knew what we were in danger of missing, and in 1967-65 we expended a good deal of adrenaline in the frenzied pursuit, by rail and road, of steam 'Up North'.

Reference will be made in a number of places in this book to PFA 800, an Austin Cambridge driven by Bill Pegg, usually with another four of us on board. The final time I was privileged to share in such a journey was on 22 July 1967, when we nipped between venues on the Settle & Carlisle (notably in the Blea Moor area) and Shap Wells on the West Coast Main Line. We published some of the photographic fruits of that day in *Moved by Steam*, but I could hardly start a chapter 'Up North' without indulging my memories of an extraordinary day very late on in the 'decline of steam'.

Back in the summer of 1965, we had paid two visits to North West England. One was on 23-24 July and we also described that visit in some detail in our previous book. However,

as indulgence seems to be the flavour of this chapter, we include two more colour shots from those days.

A couple of weeks later, I was again in the North West. In the Easter vacation of 1965 I was invited to take part in a Scripture Union Training Course for those who might help lead Christian summer camps. It was so successful that a reunion was organised by the Liverpool contingent just a few months later in Aigburth. On 19 July 1965 I made the most of my limited time by travelling out as far as Town Green and Ormskirk and capturing in colour as much as I could of the remaining steam on the Liverpool to Preston line. My attempts were not helped by the rather dull day, but it was better than nothing.

•

MIKE: We also referred briefly in *Moved by Steam* to another visit in August 1965, included a few pictures from it, and lamented the things we didn't do on that occasion. Tracking back has released a few stories of what we did do.

Opposite top What a setting! 'Jubilee' 4-6-0 No 45593 *Kolhapur* has emerged from Blea Moor Tunnel and is crossing Dent Head Viaduct with the late-running 06.35 Birmingham-Glasgow on 22 July 1967. *RNI*

Opposite Earlier on the same day, and at the same location, an unidentified Class 5 4-6-0 heads a mixed freight towards Blea Moor Tunnel. *RNI*

Above 'Exhausting' work. On 23 July 1965 Stanier '5' 4-6-0 No 44772 makes its presence felt at the head of a mixed freight through Lancaster station. The task being carried out on the left may be less strenuous, but it looks pretty risky. *RNI*

Below Refreshment for thirsty engines, though not for this one. 8F 2-8-0 No 48542 passes over Garsdale troughs with a rake of empty mineral wagons on 24 July 1965. *RNI*

The view from the north end of Ormskirk station. Fairburn 2-6-4T No 42096 creates a timeless view of a suburban stopping train as it eases its way south on 19 July 1965. The branch line to St Helens can be seen on the right of the picture. *RNI*

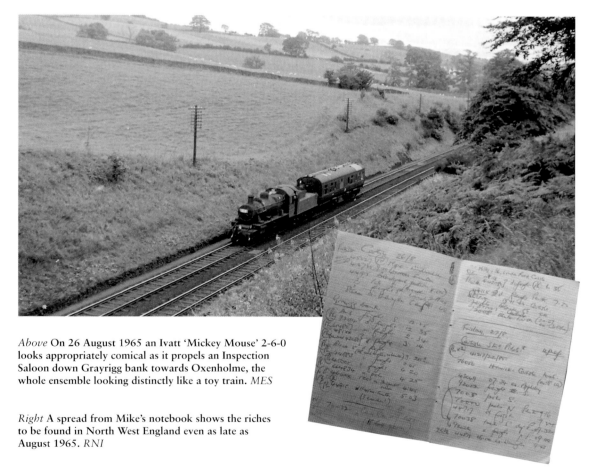

Above On 26 August 1965 an Ivatt 'Mickey Mouse' 2-6-0 looks appropriately comical as it propels an Inspection Saloon down Grayrigg bank towards Oxenholme, the whole ensemble looking distinctly like a toy train. *MES*

Right A spread from Mike's notebook shows the riches to be found in North West England even as late as August 1965. *RNI*

On Thursday 26 August I travelled from Burton-on-Trent to Preston ('cost: 1/6' according to my notebook – I hitch-hiked most of the way) where I joined the 09.50 (Tuesdays and Thursdays Only) Blackpool North-Windermere, eight coaches hauled by No 45227. In the stop of 2min 19sec at Lancaster, I ran to the booking office and bought a seven-day Rover ticket (35/-) and a local timetable, then continued with 45227 to Oxenholme for photography.

A pleasant time was rather soured when I missed a shot of No 70032 with the 15.30 relief Crewe-Glasgow. Notebook: 'No Ph O, Woe! (18 late approx)'.

An English Electric Type 4 took me to Carlisle on the 13.35 Euston-Perth. I'd booked in at Mrs Miller's B&B in London Road, so when No 72008 *Clan Macleod* took over I let it go. The scar is permanent, especially as I had to share a room with a lorry-driver who asked me increasingly personal questions, culminating in 'If I touched you, would you scream?' The answer was YES, and fortunately I heard no more from him, but for an innocent like me sleep was a long time coming.

Carlisle Station next morning felt safer; I returned to Penrith behind another Type 4, then caught the 08.35 Workington-Euston portion of the 'Lakes Express', No 42663 with three coaches to Oxenholme, and No 45342 thence to Carnforth with 11 (including the Windermere portion). But suppose I'd phoned my apologies to Mrs Miller, gone to Carstairs with No 72008, back to Carnforth, up the coast to Workington with the overnight sleeper, then with 42663 over the CKP to Penrith... If only. From Carnforth I went to Wennington on the 12.20 Carnforth-Leeds (No 42155 with three; the target signs on the closed Borwick and Arkholme stations are an abiding memory), eventually reaching Lancaster in time for the 14.43 to Glasgow (13.05 ex-Manchester, 13.10 ex-Liverpool), regularly booked for Bank Hall 'Jubilee' No 45698 *Mars*, which we'd missed on the July trip. I had planned a rendezvous at Lancaster with Richard and with our old friend and mentor the late Mike Thompson, well known in later years for his fine articles in *Steam Days*. (Mike always published under

that name, but to us he was 'Mick', and so we shall refer to him.) In the days before mobile phones, such arrangements for meeting were uncertain, and correspondingly exciting. I was there in plenty of time; Mick, hitching from Newbury (Berks), ran up the platform with seconds to spare; Richard was already aboard.

•

RICHARD: I was indeed aboard in body, if not quite in my right mind. The training course for leadership at summer camps (see above) had clearly paid off. A fortnight camped in a wonderful spot above the Devon village of Salcombe had gone well and my skills acquired had evidently included 'being a banker' and 'filling waste pits', as my diary records for Thursday 26 August 1965. For that day, and the next two, it reads as follows:

(26th Aug)
'Gave out money etc to lads and dispatched them on coaches to Totnes. Did clearing up – filled in wet pit etc (!) before leaving at 5.45pm for Kingsbridge. 7.26 off Totnes, 1.10am off Bristol. Burton arr 4.58am. [Caught the first No 10] Bus home!'
(27th Aug)
'Left on the 9.09 from Burton after a stunning 2 hours sleep. Steam Manc to Lanc where Micks [note the plural] joined the train and went to Glasgow over Shap and Beattock behind Jubilee. Great! Returned to Carlisle and thence to Skipton.'
(28th Aug)
'Caught the 0308 off Skipton again Jubilee over Aisgill. Very nice. Then 0620 to Preston ('5') and 1012 ('5') back to Carlisle. Grotty run that got banked from Oxenholme! [Actually Tebay.] Returned to Oxenholme for photos and then caught train to home via Carlisle and Leeds.'

Among other things, the diary for the next day records that I went to bed early that evening. Having not had any sleep for virtually three days, it was hardly surprising! Now Mike again takes up the story of those days, filling in the details from his logs and notebooks.

MIKE: From Lancaster, we continued with *Mars* to Glasgow, where we arrived 13 minutes late; I have no return records to Carlisle, so it must have been a diesel. As on the previous trip we hung around there until the time came to continue to Skipton with another (Sulzer rather than EE – as if we cared). No 45574 *India* took us back over the S&C with the 21.07 extra

Above All aboard! There was just time for Mike to take this portrait of 'Jubilee' No 45698 *Mars* at Lancaster before he joined Mick Thompson and Richard to travel behind it to Carlisle on 27 August 1965. *MES*

Right Fifty minutes later *Mars* is making a respectable job of the climb to Shap Summit on its regular turn, the Friday 13.05 from Manchester and 13.10 from Liverpool to Glasgow. *MES*

Logs: Lancaster and Oxenholme to Carlisle

(1) 13.05 Manchester and 13.10 Liverpool to Glasgow, 27 August 1965.

Loco: 45698. Load: 11.

(2) 16.05 Blackpool-Newcastle, 28 August 1965.

Loco: 70032. Load: 8.

(1) miles	(2) miles		(1) sched	actual	mph	(2) sched	actual	mph
0.00		LANCASTER	0	0.00	-			
3.10		Hest Bank		5.32	60			
4.45		Bolton-le-Sands		6.53	60			
6.25		Carnforth		8.47	62/60			
9.50		mp 9½		12.22	55			
13.00		mp 13		15.55	64			
13.55		Milnthorpe		16.26	64			
15.45		Hincaster Jct		18.33	51			
19.10	0.00	OXENHOLME		23.13	42	0	0.00	
24.00	4.90	mp 24		32.02	31		7.44	51
26.15	7.05	Grayrigg		36.54	27		10.28	49
27.90	8.80	Low Gill		39.45	42		12.24	59
							sigs	30*
32.10	13.00	TEBAY		45.43	47		17.44	64
35.10	16.00	Scout Green		50.27	27		21.06	41
37.55	18.45	Shap Summit		56.41	22½		25.23	35
39.70	20.60	Shap		59.45	50		27.32	64
42.90	23.80	Thrimby Grange			66/74		30.35	68
47.95	28.85	Eden Valley Jct		67.33	77		35.04	73
				pws	50*		pws	50*
51.25	32.15	PENRITH	72	71.57	-		38.24	65
4.90	37.05	Plumpton		7.15	67		42.37	77
10.55	42.70	Southwaite		12.16	80		47.12	84/74
16.45	48.60	Carlisle No 13		17.59	sigs			
16.90	49.05	Carlisle No 12					52.36	
				sig stand 2m 00s			sig stand 10m 55s	
17.85	50.00	CARLISLE	27	25.43	-	73	67.02	-
Estimated net times				71+20			52½	

from St Pancras – 72mph at Settle Junction raised our hopes, but a poor performance over the 'Long Drag' confirmed the conventional wisdom: too fast down from Hellifield means slower later.

What next? Many hours with little sleep, and a Saturday morning with miserable weather, suggested a trip to Preston on the 06.20 Carlisle-Warrington slow, returning with the 09.25 Blackpool-Glasgow (No 45328 on ten). Oh dear: 18 at Lambrigg; banked over Shap of course; 17½ minutes late into Carlisle... Back to Oxenholme, with a diesel, for pictures there.

Richard left to travel back to Burton, as his diary (above) recorded. Mick and I returned to Carlisle with No 70032, only eight on, with the 16.05 Blackpool-Newcastle. Excellent: 49 at Grayrigg, 35 at Shap Summit, 84 before Southwaite. Then, Nemesis, with a signal

Above On the thoroughly miserable morning of 28 August 1965 'Black 5' No 45328 arrives at Preston with the 09.25 Blackpool (North)-Glasgow. Our disappointing run behind it is described in the text. *RNI*

Below An ex-LMS 2-6-4 tank approaches Oxenholme in better weather with a train from Windermere in the late afternoon of the same day. *RNI*

Left 'Royal Scot' 4-6-0 No 46115 *Scots Guardsman*, the last of the class in BR service and now preserved, leaves the Settle & Carlisle line with the 15.40 Bradford-Carlisle stopper on 28 August 1965. 'Britannia' No 70032 *Tennyson*, on the 16.05 Blackpool-Newcastle with Mike and Mick aboard, is being held to let the 'Scot' into Citadel station. The picture on page 2 of *Moved by Steam* shows the opposite situation, with our 'Jubilee'-hauled train from Skipton waiting for a 'Black 5' on the Shap line. *MES*

stand of 10min 55sec outside Citadel (see the log above). According to another railwayman, the crew were only in such a hurry because they wanted to watch some important football match, presumably on TV – alas for their hopes. But for us the wait was worth it, as No 46115 *Scots Guardsman* overtook us off the S&C and allowed our last 'real' pictures of this wonderful loco, later to be preserved.

On the Sunday, I faffed about, observing No 43011 on the Morecambe-Heysham workmen's train, travelling from Morecambe to Windermere with 'Black 5' No 44964, and

photographing No 70018 *Flying Dutchman* on the unbelievable (for 1965) regular Sunday steam duty with the 'Mid-day Scot' north of Crewe.

•

RICHARD: In *Moved by Steam* we made a brief reference to a visit that Mike and I paid to Peak Forest station on 21 March 1964. No photographs of this visit were included – we

'Britannia' No 70018 *Flying Dutchman* heads into the fells above Oxenholme with the northbound 'Mid-day Scot' on Sunday 29 August 1965. *MES*

thought that the foul weather had made for rather dull pictures. However, revisiting the material in the course of the 'archaeological dig' through our catalogues for the present volume, we discovered that one or two from that visit were really quite dramatic. In the old days, experiments would have been made in the darkroom with test strips to discover the best exposure to bring out the detail from the negative. Today we have the advantage of a much easier process afforded by an electronic darkroom – Adobe Photoshop.

Mike's notebook for that day contains information from the Working Timetable, and includes the entry: '48017/44247 5K68 1.45 Tunstead ICI-Hartford (Oakleigh) Due 2.00 Actual 2.03.' A sequence of photos taken of this train is reproduced here.

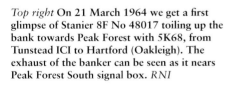

Top right **On 21 March 1964 we get a first glimpse of Stanier 8F No 48017 toiling up the bank towards Peak Forest with 5K68, from Tunstead ICI to Hartford (Oakleigh). The exhaust of the banker can be seen as it nears Peak Forest South signal box.** *RNI*

Above and right **In an age of privatisation, it's easy to forget that wagons could be owned privately under nationalisation too. Here the ownership is clearly seen as the same train passes the camera. In the right-hand picture, LMS 4F No 44247, banking tender-first, makes a substantial contribution to the common weal. The signal box (still in use to this day) is again to be seen in the distance.** *RNI*

There is still plenty of activity at Peak Forest today, but Class 60 and 66 EWS diesel locomotives don't have the attraction (for me, at any rate) of the mixture of 8Fs, 'Austerities', 9F 2-10-0s, and a miscellany of smaller engines, hauling and banking the heavy mineral wagons northwards through the station.

I revisited Peak Forest on 8 January 2011. Thanks to the dire warnings of astronomic fines from the present operators, DB Schenker, obtaining precise parallels of our archive with today's railway workings was not possible. However, a scramble along a footpath high on the eastern side of the line afforded good views of operations, including one Class 60 loco making a passable imitation of that 4F 0-6-0's exhaust!

Left The 4F 0-6-0 tracks back under the Peak Forest station road bridge. This shot also appears on the back cover of the present volume, aptly illustrating its title. *RNI*

Below Peak Forest today. On 8 January 2011 EWS Class 60 No 60039 tries to emulate the 4F as it sets off north under the same bridge. *RNI*

2
WHEN YOU'VE GOT TO GO...:
'DOWN SOUTH', 1966-63

MIKE: Although in the mid-1960s the epicentre of steam action was gradually moving northwards, there was still a fair bit to be seen elsewhere. Richard, at Oxford, was well placed to record it; I wasn't, but my interest in railway photography was now matched by an interest in timing trains, and somehow the time and money had to be found to travel on the last true steam-hauled express passenger service in Britain, between Waterloo and Bournemouth. Material in the next layer, therefore, comes from 'Down South'.

When I first drafted this chapter, I'd just received a flyer from Steam Dreams, advertising their rail tours for 2010 and saying proudly: 'As custodians of the Southern Steam experience … we will mark the end of steam on the Southern…'. That end came on 9 July 1967; alas, we weren't there. My last trips to the Southern were in 1966. During a week with my parents at Christchurch, in August, I spent

half the time trundling through the New Forest behind steam, and the other half tramping through it looking for rare plants. (That's not counting the half-hour or so trailing round Winchester Cathedral, carrying a giant teddy-bear. Well, its owner was a *very* attractive girl.) Not surprisingly, the photographic record of that trip is slight; what is surprising is that a record exists. So loose had the grip of steam become that the film stayed in its cassette without being developed, let alone printed, for some 17 years. The images are a bit thin, but it's a tribute to Ilford FP3 film and the skills of Cambridge University Library Photographic Department that anything came out at all.

However, in the two years before that,

Below **On the New Forest heaths west of Brockenhurst, Mike was able to combine his two passions, botany and railways, with unusual success. An LMS 2-6-2 tank crosses Setley Plain with the branch train for Lymington in August 1966.** *MES*

we, and I in particular, had been Down South on several occasions. Mick Thompson, who then lived at Newbury, spent a great deal of time at weekends on the Bournemouth line, photographing the Bulleids, making notes of their movements, and – above all – riding behind them. The fraternity of which he was a part had soon learned which drivers were worth following, and had got the rosters off by heart. Reports came back of the exploits of Messrs Hooper, Porter, Saunders, Sloper, Varney and Woods. It was a long way to go, but I managed to see a bit of the action.

My first term at Cambridge ended on 3 December 1965. It had been very hard work: everything I'd been told at school was called into question. And I'd never spent more than a week away from home on my own, so I was terribly homesick. On my first afternoon back I cycled out to Sutton-on-the-Hill, 8 miles north of Burton, to collect my father's glasses, left in the Methodist chapel where he'd been preaching. The Derbyshire hills already had snow on them, and I was overwhelmed with emotion for my own part of the world. I'd brought home a bagful of books to study; I finished the first one and couldn't remember a word. There could only be one cure for all this: steam! I headed Down South, for on Saturday

11 December Hooper of Nine Elms was booked for the up 'Wessy' – the 'Royal Wessex' (07.32 Weymouth-Waterloo), and Mick T.'s parents had kindly invited me to stay.

I hitch-hiked down on the 10th, the normal form of transport for students in those days. I was at Oxford in time to photograph the northbound 'Pines Express' – no longer routed by the S&DJ, alas – and was surprised to see it come in behind a 'Merchant Navy', though in fact they weren't so very uncommon there.

The 'Pacific', a pannier tank and a 'large Prairie' made me think I should have been reading English at Oxford, not steamless Cambridge, even if it had meant doing Anglo-Saxon as well…

Next morning we set out early for Winchester on Mick's scooter. In came the 'Wessy' with No 35012 *United States Lines* – a good one, and Hooper's steed on his already famous run of 4 April that year on the 'Bournemouth Belle', when Roundwood summit was cleared at 76. A heavy-faced, tough-looking bloke leaned from the cab.

'That's him,' said Mike.

Below 'Merchant Navy' No 35027 **Port Line** enters Oxford from the south with the 'Pines Express' from Bournemouth to Manchester on 10 December 1965. *MES*

Above No 35027 and the 'Pines' again: the down train stands at Basingstoke on 11 December 1965. As ever, enthusiasts are undeterred by the winter gloom. *MES*

With a start from Winchester we had less of a run at the bank than the 'Belle', and anyway that classic effort had been specially set up, with Inspector Brian Smith plying a second shovel. But 68½ was good enough for us. By that time electrification was in full swing and the run overall was infested by slacks. But thanks to Hooper's initial energy the schedule was kept almost precisely; see the accompanying logs.

The return trip, with a different driver and a light load, was devoid of interest; we stopped off at Basingstoke and noted that *Port Line* was still on the 'Pines'.

On 12 June 1965 Roger Newman and I cadged a free ride to London with a school sports team, the object being to travel to Basingstoke behind steam with the revered Driver Woods, of the Bournemouth (70F) top link. The loco was No 35023 *Holland-Afrika Line*. Two days later the revised schedules were introduced to allow for electrification work; Woods's run was already affected by the slacks, but he gained nearly 3 minutes on the old schedule, or 11 on the new!

Recording Bulleid performance was also the main aim of a week at Southampton with a Southern Region Railrover at Easter the same year. (Just as well, since my camera chose

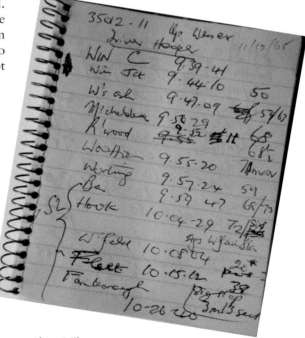

Above Mike can still feel the excitement with which he recorded these details of Driver Hooper's brilliant climb to Roundwood with the 'Royal Wessex'. A full log appears on page 29. *RNI*

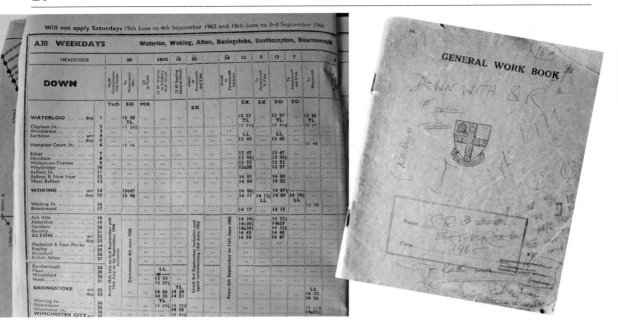

Above left This extract from a Working Timetable formerly owned by Mick Thompson shows the effect of electrification works on the Bournemouth main line. Did they really need all those extra minutes (see the text)? *RNI*

Above right This humble Burton Grammar School General Work Book was destined for greater things – recording Mike's journeys 'Down South' at Easter 1965. No doubt British Railways deserved his imprecation in general, but the immediate cause is not remembered. *RNI*

that week to develop wind-on trouble, and I have many fewer pictures than I should.) I'd been warned (by Mick T.) that I hadn't chosen the best part of the roster for drivers, but this was the best I could do in the school holidays.

A hectic week had begun with one of those desperately early starts, to Derby from Burton on the 2.30am Lincoln Mail, then to London on the Glasgow sleeper in time to catch the 8.30 Waterloo to Bournemouth (No 35007 *Aberdeen Commonwealth*, nothing special) to spend a few hours on the S&D at Blandford Forum. I finally staggered back to Southampton on the 6.40pm ex-Bournemouth (Driver Shepherd of Eastleigh, No 34082, good,

Log: Waterloo to Basingstoke			
13.30 Waterloo-Weymouth, 12 June 1965.			
Driver: Woods (Bournemouth). Loco: 35023. Load: 12.			
miles		sched	actual	mph
0.00	WATERLOO	0	0.00	-
1.30	Vauxhall		3.47	37
3.90	CLAPHAM JCT	7	7.20	51/47
7.20	WIMBLEDON		11.16	62
9.75	New Malden		13.45	65
12.05	SURBITON		15.45	68
13.35	*Hampton Court Jct*	18	16.55	70
17.10	Walton-on-Thames		19.50	76/74
19.10	Weybridge		21.33	78
21.65	West Byfleet		23.33	76/74
24.30	WOKING	27½**	25.43	71
28.00	Brookwood		28.48	69/71
31.00	*mp, 31*		pws	41*
33.25	Farnborough		34.39	
36.50	Fleet		38.39	54*
39.85	Winchfield		42.01	54*
42.20	Hook		44.29	63
			sigs	
47.80	BASINGSTOKE	55	52.12	-
Estimated net time 47 minutes			
* Speed restriction			
** Schedule to Woking Junction			

Left On 23 April 1965 another 'Merc', probably No 35028 *Clan Line*, is about to take water at Southampton Central before departing, under the famous gantry and past the dockland cranes, with what is believed to be the 8.30am Waterloo-Weymouth. The young gentleman has the air of a 'regular' – someone may recognise him. *MES*

74 after Beaulieu Road) for the first of several nights at the YMCA Hostel. *Not* good – a neighbour had a noisy radio – so I was even more shattered the next day…

On 21 April I was joined by Mick and other members of the Southern gang for what looked like being the one really bright spot of the week – the 12.40pm Bournemouth-Waterloo with Jack Varney, the other star turn of 70F. Mick had told me of a splendid earlier trip with Varney where a defect on the loco at Southampton had been cured by a piece of string, and a French passenger, wishing

Below Standard Class 5 No 73051 arrives at Blandford Forum southbound with a Somerset & Dorset line train on 20 April 1965. *MES*

to congratulate 'Monsieur le mécanicien' on arrival at Waterloo, had some difficulty in seeing a giant of the footplate in this slightly scruffy little bloke. Ignore appearances: our run was the work of a great man throughout and a completely clear road allowed Mr Varney to give a magisterial performance. A fast exit from Southampton, no flogging of the engine, and a modest 59 at Roundwood secured a gain of 5½ minutes to Worting. There was no sense of haste – the line speed of 85 was never exceeded – but we were into Waterloo exactly 7 minutes early, with the fastest time the guard had ever recorded. Comparison with Hooper's run is difficult, given all the checks

Below In another picture from 23 April 1965 No 35022 *Holland-America Line* is in the middle of a strange manoeuvre that until 1970 was executed by all up trains calling at Dorchester South. It has arrived from Weymouth via the curve on the left and has backed into the former terminus; it now waits to leave for Bournemouth. Also curious, but quite usual, is the ratio of power to load: surely no British railway other than the Southern and its BR successor ever expended so much 'Pacific' haulage on trains of around 170 tons (or often less)? *MES*

he experienced, but each is a finely judged response to the prevailing conditions.

After that the runs got steadily worse and I decided to spend much of the rest of my stay photographing. The weather was mixed for my full day in Dorset, but by the time I got to Corfe Castle it was a beautiful late afternoon. Pictures of the castle are a must for tourists, and pictures from it and from the neighbouring East Hill are a must for railway photographers, with their backgrounds of the village, the viaduct, the station, and the Purbeck Hills. Of course, that's when the wind-on went wrong. That Law again… What's more, I got locked into the castle, and on jumping down from the exit gate gave myself an injury (which took months to heal) in an unmentionable place… It's a good job for the Department of Works that H&S hadn't been invented.

Saturday on the Isle of Wight produced no pictures at all, but by Sunday the camera was constipated rather than occluded. On that day engineering work had caused a diversion of Southampton-Waterloo trains

		Logs: Southampton and Winchester to Waterloo						

(1) 11.25 Weymouth-Waterloo, 21 April 1965.

Driver: Varney (Bournemouth). Loco: 35007. Load: 11.

(2) 07.32 Weymouth-Waterloo, 11 December 1965.

Driver: Hooper (Nine Elms). Loco: 35012. Load: 11.

(1) miles	(2) miles		(1) sched	actual	mph	(2) sched	actual	mph
0.00		SOUTHAMPTON C	0	0.00	-			
1.05		*Northam Jct*	3½	3.45	31/15*			
1.95		St Denys		5.31	46			
3.45		Swaythling		7.20	52			
5.70		EASTLEIGH	10	9.31	62			
9.50		Shawford		13.06	66/67			
12.65	0.00	WINCHESTER C		15.57	65/67	0	0.00	-
14.75	2.10	*Winchester Jct*	20½	17.55	64/66	5	4.29	50
21.15	8.50	Micheldever		23.57	61		10.48	68
23.00	10.35	*Roundwood*		25.21	59		12.30	68½
28.95	16.30	*Worting Jct*	37	31.47	60	24½	17.43	59
31.45	18.80	BASINGSTOKE		34.05	77/83		20.06	68/73
37.05	24.40	Hook		38.03	82/79		24.48	72
							pws, sigs	
39.40	26.75	Winchfield		40.09	78		28.23	20*
42.75	30.10	Fleet		42.39	84/75		35.21	38*
							sig stand 3m 13s	
46.00	33.35	Farnborough		45.23	73		46.59	
48.25	35.60	*m.p. 31*		47.15	72/73		49.52	
51.25	38.60	Brookwood		49.48	69/71		52.39	72
54.95	42.30	WOKING	58½**	52.55	70/74	57½**	56.23	sigs
57.60	44.95	West Byfleet		55.15	72		60.07	
60.15	47.50	Weybridge		57.20	71		62.47	60
62.15	49.50	Walton-on-Thames		58.59	70/76		64.47	67
65.90	53.25	*Hampton Court Jct*	67½	62.00	75	67	67.50	78***
67.20	54.55	SURBITON		63.03	72		68.50	80
69.50	56.85	New Malden		64.56	68		70.46	60
72.05	59.40	WIMBLEDON		67.13	69/65		73.29	35* pws
75.35	62.70	CLAPHAM JCT	77	70.46	35*	76½	77.49	
77.95	65.30	Vauxhall		74.08	39			
79.25	66.60	WATERLOO	84	77.00	-	83½	83.49	-
Estimated net times			77			64		

* Speed restriction

** Schedule to Woking Junction

*** Speed at Esher

to the Portsmouth Direct line via Havant. I chose *not* to travel with Bulleids over Buriton summit, and it's still on my wish list; a few nice shots in the Rowland's Castle area are some compensation.

Until not long before, a number of steam-worked Southern Region branches had survived in Surrey and Sussex. One of the

Above With the Distant signal at 'caution', a rebuilt Bulleid 'light Pacific' has shut off steam and passes the disused Monkton & Came Halt on the approach to Dorchester with an up express on 23 April 1965. The nameplate looks unusual and a friend has suggested that this may be 'BB' No 34090 *Sir Eustace Missenden, Southern Railway. MES*

Below The Master Shot meets Murphy's Law. What should have been an ideal image of trains passing at Corfe Castle on 23 April 1965 has been unideally cropped by a faulty wind-on. Still, the little station, with the 2-6-2 tank blowing off, looks charming against the dip slope of the Purbeck Hills. *MES*

few still there in 1965, and soon to go, was Guildford to Horsham, so on the last day of my holiday I paid my respects. I must have been tired, for even the pictures produce no memory of what was obviously a delightful area.

Steam between Reading and Redhill, however, had already finished on 4 January, and trips to that lovely line had become a matter of urgency for both of us the previous year. Bag that 'Q'! Ride behind those 'Moguls'!

Above Lineside cowslips revel in the chalk soil of the South Downs as rebuilt 'West Country' No 34001 *Exeter* climbs past Finchdean, on the Portsmouth Direct line, with a diverted Southampton Docks-Waterloo boat train on Sunday 26 April 1965. *MES*

Below Baynards station, on the Surrey/Sussex border, was originally built to serve the local Great House, but for much of its life served little more than the local pub. Its setting deep in ancient woodland is suggested by this shot of LMS 2-6-2 tank No 41294 approaching the crossing point from the single line with an afternoon Horsham-Guildford train on 26 April 1965. The driver looks more like a commuter than a railwayman... *MES*

Snap that Southern station! Dig that North Downs scenery!

The day after my visit, Saturday 1 August 1964, was spent at Farnborough and Woking with Mick T. and friends. There was something not quite right about the LSWR main line. Four tracks, lots of it dead straight, regimented trees, low cuttings... And, of course, the motive power was rather lacking in variety; but my goodness me what a lot of it there was! On page 35 a spread from my notebook shows what we saw that day. This was the last Summer timetable with a proper Southern-style service to Exeter and beyond, before the Western began their triumphant downgrading of the route. So never mind if a bit of imagination was needed to give excitement to the day, or to the pictures: we have the record, and what we'd give for such a day now!

Right, below and opposite On 28 November 1964, with little more than a month to go before the end of steam on the Reading-Redhill line, a pilgrimage was *de rigueur*, whatever the weather. 'N' 2-6-0 No 31408, her fireman and her train stand out sharply against a misty, moisty landscape as they head eastwards, below the Way used by earlier pilgrims, with Richard aboard.

Alighting at Dorking Town and shooting from the hip, he bagged the 'N' again, this time with her driver, before sprinting to the next overbridge for two final shots. *All RNI*

Above Mike's visit to the Reading-Redhill line was on a warm but hazy summer's day, 31 July 1964. In the first of these two pictures, and looking even more than usual like a copy of a Fowler 4F, 'Q' 0-6-0 No 30543 of Redhill stands at Sandhurst Halt with a train for Reading. *MES*

Below Heading towards its home town of Guildford, another 'N', No 31800, arrives at Dorking Town. *MES*

9836

2nd. DAY RETURN

Dorking (Town)

to

GUILDFORD

(S)   Fare 5/0

For conditions see over

BRITISH TRANSPORT COMMISSION

VALID DAY OF ISSUE

Issued subject to the Regulations and Conditions in the Commission's Publications and Notices applicable to British Railways

NOT TRANSFERABLE

Below right Like the lines featured in Chapter 5, that from Waterloo to Basingstoke was one where you just waited and it all went by. This spread from Mike's notebook shows the sheer abundance of steam-hauled traffic on a summer Saturday in 1964. *RNI*

Bottom and overleaf Saturday 1 August 1964: Bulleid 'Pacifics' on the LSW main line, in the last summer of full steam working to the West of England. 'Merchant Navy' No 35006 *Peninsular & Oriental S. N. Co*, passing Woking with the 1.00pm Waterloo-Ilfracombe, looks like a stationary exhibit; in fact the day was too hot at that hour for any steam to show. The picture also makes us

think of a famous episode in Jerome K. Jerome's *Three Men in a Boat*. The three travellers arrive at Waterloo and are unable to find their train, but eventually locate one whose driver is willing – for half a crown – to go to Kingston as the 11.05. They discover later that it 'was really the Exeter mail, and that they had spent hours at Waterloo looking for it, and that nobody knew what had become of it.' The quantity of information on No 35006's smokebox suggests that the staff of Nine Elms wished for no repetition of this episode. *MES*

Left and below These two pictures show a characteristic stretch of line east of Farnborough, with rebuilt 'West Country' No 34048 *Crediton* on the 8.46am Salisbury-Waterloo and unrebuilt 'Battle of Britain' No 34057 *Biggin Hill* on the 10.35am Waterloo-Padstow. *Both MES*

Below Later in the day, the 'Royal Wessex' (4.35pm Waterloo-Weymouth), complete with headboard, passes the same spot behind 'Merchant Navy' No 35021 *New Zealand Line*. *MES*

In 1963 Mick's parents had accommodated Richard and me for the Southern Region Summer Shed-bash (see *Moved by Steam*), but they'd also had the dubious pleasure of my company for a few days at Easter. Of course there had to be an Eastleigh visit, and there was one to Swindon too – some more of the results can be seen in Chapter 6. But from both there are mementoes of the Southern main line, and perhaps more valuably of the Western, where Richard, lucky man, was able to record the last gasps two years or so later.

•

RICHARD: I completed my course at Oxford in the summer of 1968. Steam had long gone from Oxford by then. I recently asked Liz,

Above 'S15' 4-6-0 No 30499 is on a down parcels at Basingstoke on 15 August 1963. *MES*

Right On the same day we were able to secure from the train (shown overleaf) a charming portrait of vintage Adams LSWR 'B4' 0-4-0T No 30096 on its regular shunting job at Winchester. *MES*

Above **Having alighted shortly afterwards at Eastleigh, we watched our train restart behind Standard Class 5 No 73083** *Pendragon. MES*

Right **On 15 April 1963 ex-GWR 'Mogul' No 6344 stands at Newbury with an up local.** *MES*

married to me for 41 years, to cast her mind back to 1967 – the year we started to 'go out'. Had I disappeared from time to time to the railway? Her memory is much sharper than mine for things that long ago, but she cannot recall any such occasion. For my increased availability Liz can thank the withdrawal of long-distance passenger services from the former Great Central Railway on 4 September 1966. That in turn meant the end of the last steam passenger working through the city, the

Bournemouth-York (by then, strictly speaking, the Poole-York), now diverted via Birmingham with diesel power. Even before that, with the closure of Oxford shed on 3 January, the 'Halls' had disappeared; there was still the occasional Bulleid 'Pacific', but 'Black 5s' were normally in charge. While I was brought up on

Above 'Castle' No 7018 *Drysllwyn Castle*, famous for its record-breaking run on the up 'Bristolian' in 1958, is carrying Class 'A' headlamps at Reading on 17 April 1963, but may in fact be on station pilot duty. *MES*

Below The GW 'small Prairies' always looked pleasing, and pleased with themselves, and were nearly always well turned out. No 5569, of the later series with bevelled side tanks, passes Swindon with a freight on 18 April 1963. *MES*

the London Midland Region, and so had rather a soft spot for that large and sometimes under-estimated class of locos, it just wasn't the same.

In retrospect, the spring and summer of 1965, with their seemingly endless sunshine and the 'Halls' still working, were the halcyon days of my time in Oxford as far as steam was concerned. One particularly memorable occasion was on 22 May 1965, when Andrew Dow, Robert Wade and I journeyed to Banbury behind 'Modified Hall' No 6980 *Llanrumney Hall*. The front cover of *Moved by Steam* depicted that departure from Oxford. Our arrival in Banbury gave us the opportunity of some further steam photography in a different setting as we awaited our return journey.

Below 'Black 5' 4-6-0 No 4469?, looking as miserable as the weather, is ready to head north from Oxford with the Bournemouth-York, probably in 1966. A Class 47 diesel can be seen in the sidings. *RNI*

In Oxford itself there were a number of locations within cycling distance of the colleges and, sometimes alone and sometimes with others, I visited many of them in that splendid summer, not only for the Bournemouth-York, but also for steam-operated freight and steam station pilots.

The weather made that a wonderful time for savouring the last of steam through Oxford in colour. (At university, while some folk spent what little was left of their grants on beer and skittles, I spent mine on colour film.) However, I also managed to capture the atmosphere of an earlier age during my first term there (October to Christmas 1964) in black and white.

CHEAP DAY - 2nd

Oxford to

BANBURY
GENERAL

(W)

7209

For conditions see over

Ticket to ride: railway enthusiasts often didn't leave the station at their destinations, allowing the outward portion of the ticket to be retained for inspection 45 years later! This square of cardboard brings back happy memories of 22 May 1965 (see the text). *RNI*

Above **Apart from the missing name and number plates, this 'Hall' presents an attractive appearance at the head of a northbound fitted freight at Banbury on 22 May 1965.** *RNI*

Right **A 'Hall' 4-6-0 awaits the road at Oxford as an unidentified Stanier 2-6-0 drifts through with a southbound freight.** *RNI*

A pannier tank moves to its next duty as station pilot while a 'large Prairie' hauls a southbound mixed freight through the central road. Diesel multiple units in the up and down platforms await their passengers. *RNI*

Above We may not know which 'Hall' this is, but we do know where someone thinks it belongs! It has a clear road ahead with its rake of mineral wagons. *RNI*

Below GW engine, SR stock – it has to be the York-Bournemouth. A 'Hall' glides into Oxford station while a DMU awaits its departure for the Kingham line in the bay platform in the summer of 1965. *RNI*

Then and now: an unidentified 'Hall' heads north out of Oxford with the Bournemouth-York in early November 1964, then on 16 September 2010 a DMU crosses the same side-channel of the River Isis, but the signal box, signal gantry and the sign saying 'Abbey Road' on the house on the right have all disappeared, though the lighter area of brickwork in the modern shot indicates where the latter used to be. *Both RNI*

South of Oxford station the tracks crossed the River Isis, and it was possible to get access to the trackside from below the bridge. The drama of this viewpoint was oddly enhanced by the gasholders that dominated the spot. 'West Country' No 34024 *Tamar Valley* hurries towards Bournemouth in October 1964. *Both RNI*

Further south still, near New Hinksey, a rather unusual footbridge, almost like a causeway, crosses a lake – clearly visible in the 1964 photographs – then climbs high above the railway to give access to South Hinksey, on the other side of the line. This vantage point afforded a bird's-eye view of approaching and retreating trains. While 45 years of tree growth is very evident in the present-day photographs, the bridge, the lake and the general layout of the track are virtually unchanged. 'West Country' Class Bulleid 'Pacific' No 34044 *Woolacombe* brings the Bournemouth-York towards Oxford one day in the period 20-28 November 1964 and disappears towards the dominant gasholders (now demolished, with no trace remaining). *Both RNI*

Above A 'Voyager', looking static compared with its steam predecessors, journeys towards Oxford on 16 September 2010. *RNI*

On 16 September 2010 another 'Voyager' leaves Oxford on the up slow. The spire of Nuffield College is still just visible to the right of possibly the same large trees in the 1964 shot opposite. *RNI*

Left **With New Hinksey in the background, 'Hall' Class 4-6-0 No 4959 *Purley Hall* makes its way north on the same day in November 1964, with a substantial train of wagons, which may well be empties.** *RNI*

Below **Oxford on a wet and cold 17 March 1964 finds 'Hall' No 6937 *Conyngham Hall* waiting for time in the northbound platform.** *RNI*

I started my Chemistry degree in Oxford in October 1964. However, the bizarre ritual of Preliminary Exams (before one even started studying there!) meant that March 1964 saw me in Oxford for that purpose. To add to the misery, it was a cold and snowy – then a cold and wet – few days. But on 17 March I spent a little time at Oxford station. En route to Oxford on the 15th I took the shot reproduced on the title page, which records the furthest date to which I can track back for steam at Oxford.

3
THE RIGHT PLACE AT THE RIGHT TIME: 'OUT WEST', 1964

RICHARD: When I was Rector of Yeovil in the early 1990s, people from the North or the Home Counties would say, 'How nice to live in the West Country! How nice to be so close to Cornwall for holidays!' When I pointed out that it was another 4 hours' drive from Yeovil into the heart of Cornwall, they began to realise that there is a lot of west 'Out West'. So perhaps, in this chapter, a definition is called for. For our purposes, we have drawn an arbitrary line from the Wirral due south down through the Welsh Marches, then looping east to include Gloucester, Bath and Templecombe, before continuing south and terminating in Lyme Bay. Everything to the west of this line is Out West.

This thick stratum accumulated during a short period, so for it the reverser moves into forward gear. In 1964 we made a number of trips to that wonderful slice of countryside between Gloucester and Hereford, and spent some time chasing a symbol of a bygone age of railways, the 'Chalford Auto'. Excursions to Mid and West Wales, to the section of the Somerset & Dorset north of Templecombe and to such glories of Devon as the Barnstaple line and the Torrington-Halwill branch were all crammed into that year. There was still much to see Out West, but we knew it couldn't last long. That didn't just apply to steam haulage; many of the lines themselves were threatened with closure. And for me it seemed important to do as much as possible in this part of my life before the great rite of passage of starting university – for which see Chapter 2.

Our first westbound trip of the year was in the gloom of January, and the second in the torrential rain (showers? huh!) of April. My diary for the January visit was optimistic: 'Did Gloucester-Hereford branch. Single line smashing phots branch', while the entry for 4 April is wonderfully understated: 'Went on the 7.12 and did the Chalford Auto. Had a good day though the weather was only mediocre.' Mike did manage to pay a third pilgrimage in September sunshine, but while I was writing this chapter at the end of 2010 my youngest daughter gave me a copy of *Steam World* for January 2011, complete with its complimentary calendar of photos by Roy Hobbs. He visited the line in June 1964, and the glorious photo of the Chalford Auto with 'our' No 1472 reproduced in the calendar just rubs salt in the wound. But let's be kind and call ours 'atmospheric'…

We've remarked before on the remarkable long-suffering of our parents around this time. Both my parents and Mike's put up with an extra teenage lad on holiday with them. In May 1964 my family had a holiday at Shaldon on the South Devon coast and Mike came too. Maybe my parents thought that the only way to get an 18-year-old away with them was (i) to pay for accommodation, (ii) to allow a friend to come too and (iii) to go somewhere attractive from a railway point of view.

First stop for steam was on a family excursion by car. Just by chance *(sic!)* we were able to get some photos at Gunnislake on the Bere Alston-Callington branch. It was a glorious day. Glorious days mean no sky in

Above On 25 January 1964 we dash to board the 12.25pm Gloucester-Hereford after a quick stop for photography at Blaisdon Halt, with ex-GWR 'large Prairie' 2-6-2T No 4107 in charge. *RNI*

Below Blaisdon Halt again – this time GWR 'Mogul' No 7307 (but with no smokebox plates) drifts in with the Gloucester-bound train, due to arrive there at 3.58pm. *MES*

Right GWR 0-4-2T No 1472, with steam apparently coming from every orifice, prepares to leave Gloucester Central with the 'Chalford Auto' on 4 April 1964. *RNI*

Right The same loco makes an enthusiastic start away from Brimscombe later that day. *RNI*

Below Between Brimscombe and Chalford an 0-4-2T propels its stock on a return journey to Gloucester. As the end nears for the 'Auto', the canal in the foreground is a reminder that transport systems have come and gone throughout history, each leaving some nostalgia of its own. *MES*

Above That's more like it! The weather was much kinder for Mike's trip on 12 September 1964, and the sun is setting in both senses on the Gloucester-Hereford line. Here GWR 0-6-0PT No 4623 pulls up late in the afternoon at Blaisdon Halt to allow Mike and A. N. Other to board. *MES*

Below A last lingering look at the 'Chalford Auto' as it sets out from Gloucester on 12 September 1964. By early November it would be running no more. *MES*

black and white photos – but the situation of the station with its backdrop of wonderful rolling Devon countryside made up for it. Regrets? Yes, as always. I still wasn't shooting in colour – what an opportunity missed.

The next day was a full-blown railway outing. We went from Teignmouth to Exeter and thence to Templecombe via the SR. A change on to the S&D and we went north up the line to Evercreech. This gave the chance

Ivatt 2-6-2T No 41291 approaches Gunnislake on the afternoon of 19 May 1964 with a train for Callington, then waits to pass the returning service to Bere Alston, hauled by another Ivatt 2-6-2T, No 41316. *Both MES*

of photos both on the S&D proper and on its Highbridge spur. A trip from Templecombe to Salisbury and back, with a fine run from Salisbury to Exeter behind 'Spamcan' No 34086 *219 Squadron*, meant a late, but worthwhile, end to the day by the time we returned to Teignmouth.

For our second major expedition we chose to go to Honiton and Sidmouth Junction three days later. The weather couldn't have been more of a contrast as the diary says, 'Spent the day at Honiton in the very miserable rain. Stuff seen was very reasonable despite the weather.' I alone took well over a roll of film; sadly many

Nine-Elms-stabled rebuilt 'Merchant Navy' 'Pacific' No 35012 *United States Line* waits at Exeter Central with an up express – the 10.30am to Waterloo – on 20 May 1964. The gentleman bent over by his suitcase must be hoping for some help from the approaching porter. *RNI*

Above and below **Coming and going: the now preserved LMS 4F 0-6-0 No 44422 heads its three coaches north out of Evercreech Junction on the S&D line towards Bath on 20 May 1964. Mike is seen in the second shot, not about to leap aboard, but seeking a dramatic location for his photograph.** *Both RNI*

of the photos are just dross, but from our joint efforts a few both give the flavour of the day and have their own charm.

Bill Pegg's luxurious PFA 800 was introduced in Chapter 1. Three friends and I were the fortunate passengers for two trips to the Cambrian. Bill seemed more interested in driving the Austin Cambridge than in the trains we went to see, so he was able to have the engine revved up and ready to go whenever and wherever we wanted to chase a train to another viewpoint. My diary entry for 25 July

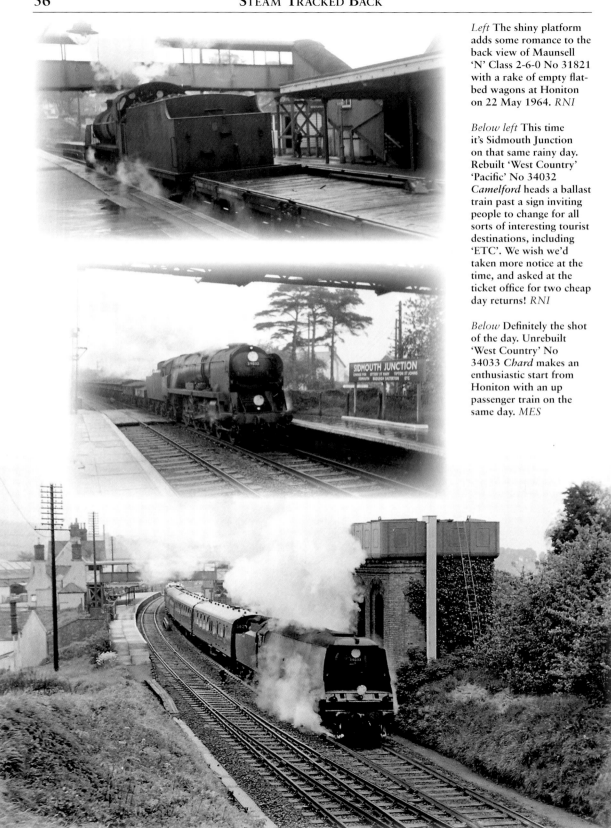

Left The shiny platform adds some romance to the back view of Maunsell 'N' Class 2-6-0 No 31821 with a rake of empty flat-bed wagons at Honiton on 22 May 1964. *RNI*

Below left This time it's Sidmouth Junction on that same rainy day. Rebuilt 'West Country' 'Pacific' No 34032 *Camelford* heads a ballast train past a sign inviting people to change for all sorts of interesting tourist destinations, including 'ETC'. We wish we'd taken more notice at the time, and asked at the ticket office for two cheap day returns! *RNI*

Below Definitely the shot of the day. Unrebuilt 'West Country' No 34033 *Chard* makes an enthusiastic start from Honiton with an up passenger train on the same day. *MES* again errs on the bright side in describing the weather as 'so-so'. However, we must have thought the whole expedition worthwhile, as on 8 August the same crew set off again.

Only a week later, Mike and I were back Out West, and this time for a full fortnight.

The first week was through the generosity of Mike's parents, who booked a holiday for us all in Ilfracombe. For this week we purchased a Holiday Runabout Ticket for 'Area No 7' of the West Country.

Same day, same locomotive and train, different location: west of Newtown on 25 July 1964 our 'chauffeur' overtook 'Manor' Class 4-6-0 No 7810 *Draycott Manor* on a westbound holiday express while it waited to cross an eastbound service. *Both RNI*

Top Our 'transport of delight', Austin Cambridge 2-2-0 PFA 800, is seen on the extreme right of this shot as 'Manor' No 7821 *Ditcheat Manor* climbs the bank near Talerddig on 8 August 1964. *RNI*

Above We understand that, in movie-making, rain machines are employed to ensure there is sufficient water to register on the film. No such artificial aids were needed on 8 August 1964 at Cemmes Road as the rain teemed down on an unidentified Standard 2-6-4T. Note another iconic 1960s road vehicle, a Hillman Minx. *RNI*

Left Perhaps Richard's favourite shot in the book! No 7824 *Iford Manor* seems to part the foliage for its train on the Cambrian line near Talerddig on 8 August 1964. By this stage in the day the rain had eased off and there was even a little sunshine. *RNI*

This is the Seat Regulation Ticket No 0065. These (free) tickets were mandatory for our journey on IV53 on Saturday 15 August 1964. Joining this train at Birmingham Snow Hill for our journey 'Out West' was to ensure steam traction for a substantial part thereof. Mike and I, together with his long-suffering parents, had had a very early start from Burton to make the connection. It's doubtful that either of your authors actually sat in their seats for any length of time! *RNI*

Having finished its duty on IV53, 'Castle' Class No 7011 *Banbury Castle* runs through Bristol Temple Meads. *RNI*

The essence of steam days: lots of mail bags on platform ends; lots of spotters; lots of barrows; and the odd passenger. In the distance, 'Grange' Class 4-6-0 No 6856 *Stowe Grange* leaves Bristol Temple Meads on the 8.30am Paignton-Manchester on Saturday 15 August 1964. *RNI*

A quick dash to the back of our train (still IV53) afforded this portrait of Churchward 'Mogul' 4MT No 7320, which passed us at Wiveliscombe. There are glimpses of Somerset countryside beyond. *RNI*

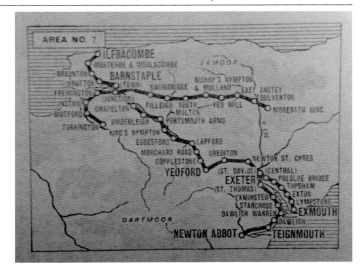

What a bargain! £1 2s 6d for the freedom of north-west and central Devon for a fortnight, coast to coast. You wouldn't believe that signature is of an 18-year-old! More like an 8-year-old's... *Both RNI*

Near Mortehoe & Woolacombe Maunsell 'N' Class 4-6-0 No 31834 leads its three carriages towards Ilfracombe on 19 August 1964. *RNI*

We observed a proper Sabbath, but then the week became distinctly active, with much use of our legs as well as the indispensable ticket. One day saw us walking with Jessie and Eric, Mike's parents, from Wrafton to Braunton Burrows, where we enjoyed the wild landscape of the dunes, and their rare flora. On another, we visited some school friends of mine who had taken jobs as waiters for the summer at a hotel in Mortehoe. I remember one of them saying he had worn out a pair of shoes in just a few weeks on the hotel carpets! We came away feeling that earning money wasn't everything in life, especially when there was summer steam to see.

Towards the end of the week we had a splendid day on the Torrington to Halwill branch. The weather was perfect, and the motive power all steam.

Then, on the last day of our stay in Ilfracombe, we travelled on the lovely Barnstaple-Taunton for the fourth, and as it turned out our final, time; it was dieselised that autumn and closed two years later.

Below At Halwill station on the same day 'N' Class 2-6-0 No 31837 awaits departure on a Padstow-Okehampton train. *RNI*

Above Forty-seven years later our memories were a bit hazy on which Halt was which on the Torrington-Halwill branch. World Wide Web to the rescue! We found some photographs of the stations long after the line had closed, and one showed Dunsbear Halt in the 1980s. In our picture a catena of wire can be seen just under the roof of the station building. The same wire was still there 20 years later! Result! On 20 August 1964 Ivatt 2-6-2T No 41208 pauses there on its journey to Halwill. *RNI*

Below By comparison with our Holiday Runabout ticket, the day trip from Torrington to Halwill and back at 7/- looks positively expensive. Maybe it included a contribution to the wage of the clerk who had to write it out! *RNI*

We have boarded the Halwill to Torrington train for the return journey. While we wait, Standard Class 4 2-6-4T No 80038 approaches with a parcels train, and, as it passes, we glimpse in the distance another of the same class approaching from the north – a good deal of traffic for a line with not long to go. *Both RNI*

Above **GWR 'Mogul' No 6363** (with the stock for its passenger duty to Taunton) shunts a parcels van at Barnstaple Junction on 21 August 1964. *RNI*

Below Freed from its shunting duties, No 6363 brings its train into the platform at Barnstaple Junction. Waiting in the station is Ivatt 2-6-2T No 41223 on a freight consisting of no more than one wagon and one brake-van. *MES*

Above Sadly (at one level) the ride back to Ilfracombe from Barnstaple Junction on 21 August 1964 was in a diesel multiple unit, but it was one of those 1960s sets that allowed a driver's-eye view through the cab. Here we pass a bunker-first 2MT 2-6-2T on a local train. During the ride we noticed beside the driver a thick volume that looked like a Working Timetable. In fact, it was an abstrusely-titled treatise on psychology. Our respect for the staff of the Western Region increased from that day forward! *RNI*

On Saturday 22 August we moved on to the next stage of our epic pilgrimage Out West. An 'N' Class 2-6-0 took us to Exeter from Barnstaple Junction, then we travelled to Bristol via Templecombe and the S&DJR. There are a number of places in Britain where the old railway company lines cross with hardly a recognition of each other's existence. For me, the high and low levels at Lichfield Trent Valley and Tamworth (see Chapter 5), the level crossing at Newark and where the S&DJR goes under the LSWR at Templecombe (see page 66) bring back special memories. Our visit on this occasion was made even more special by the wonderful weather. As we journeyed close to the Somerset Levels and over the Mendips, both were seen to perfection. Approaching Bath Green Park through Devonshire Tunnel,

we ran through the parish of Bath, St Luke. Little did I realise that 20 years later I would spend eight years ministering there – and walk with three daughters along that same trackbed!

A 'Freedom of Wales' Railrover Ticket set us back 5 guineas. (Remember guineas?) This felt like a king's ransom in those days, but I have an (unreliable?) memory that parents again came to the rescue with a 'sub'.

Our largely steamless journey through South Wales was diversified by a glimpse of the Severn Tunnel car-ferry service and a visit to the Barry scrapyard. From Carmarthen to Aberystwyth we travelled behind a 'Standard 4' 2-6-4 tank on a mixed passenger and milk train, and another of the same class brought us to Machynlleth for the night.

Above Visible in Templecombe loco yard on 22 August 1964 are ex-S&D 2-8-0 No 53807 and Collett 0-6-0 No 2217, and a Ford Anglia, an Austin Cambridge, and what might be a Standard van. Templecombe Junction signal box can be seen in the distance. *RNI*

Below Standard Class 4 2-6-0 No 76027 approaches Templecombe Lower Platform with a train for Bath Green Park on 22 August 1964. Mike can be glimpsed at the bottom of the picture, going for (but not in fact taking) the 'looming loco' shot. *RNI*

On the same day, since-preserved 4F No 44422 stops at Evercreech Junction – which, like others on the S&D, looked like a country cottage that just happened to be by the railway. In this less usual shot, 44422 sets off past the water tower and level crossing gates on the next step of its journey to Bath Green Park. Notice the attractive dip in the line near the vanishing point of the perspective. *RNI*

Below Standard Class 3 2-6-2T No 82001 is ready to leave Bath Green Park. Mercifully the lovely station canopy has been preserved, though now adjacent to the Sainsbury's supermarket car park. *RNI*

Above In the days before the Severn road bridges, the GWR, and its successor BR(WR), operated a car-ferry service through the famous tunnel, from Pilning to Severn Tunnel Junction. Our DMU passes 'large Prairie' No 4156 near Pilning with the accompanying passenger coaches (but no cars) on Sunday 23 August 1964. *MES*

Above inset Not paid for with 5 golden guineas, though the 'Freedom of Wales' ticket was a substantial slice of our budget. *Both RNI*

By now we had been joined by two other school friends, Cliff and Roger, for our continuing Welsh odyssey, and next day we all set off on a trip to Welshpool and Oswestry, with some time spent at the junction station for the Llanfyllin branch, Llanymynech.

Having had two trips earlier in the year to Talerddig, Cliff and I decided that Barmouth

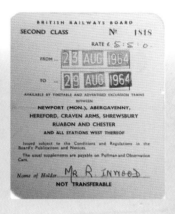

Above Between Carmarthen and Aberystwyth on 24 August 1964 our mixed passenger and milk train was hauled by Standard Class 4 2-6-4T No 80101. *RNI*

Main picture Two 'Manors' at Welshpool on 25 August 1964: No 7820 *Dinmore Manor* waits in the bay platform with the 10.10am to Whitchurch, while No 7827 *Lydham Manor* arrives and departs from the through platform with the 7.35am Aberystwyth-Shrewsbury. *RNI*

and its environs were a better bet for the lovely weather that greeted us on the morning of 26 August. Mike, however, having not been on those previous visits, spent the day with Roger on the Machynlleth to Welshpool section. As Mike and I collaborate on our series of books

45 years later, it turns out that that division of photographic labour has paid dividends!

No such division of labour the next day, as Mike and I elected for a trip to Bangor, and from there we had a return trip to Chester, headed both ways by 'Black 5s'. We also caught

Above 'Manor' 4-6-0 No 7821 *Ditcheat Manor* runs north through Llanymynech with a mixed freight on 25 August 1964. *RNI*

Below Smartly dressed passengers alight from an arrival on the northbound platform at Barmouth on 26 August 1964. Standard Class 3 2-6-2T No 82006 is in charge. *RNI*

Above What a location! 'Manor' Class 4-6-0 No 7816 *Frilsham Manor* adds to the elegance of the terrace of houses as it drifts south of Barmouth station with a fitted freight on 26 August 1964. *RNI*

Below From elegance to the sublime: on the approach to the bridge over Afon Mawddach, the backdrop is that iconic mountain, Cader Idris. The driver, however, prefers the view out to sea. *RNI*

some steam from Afon Wen to Bangor later in the day, and eventually met up with Rog and Cliff again when we arrived in Harlech for the night. There is a vague memory of the four of us playing primary-school-style war games on the dunes. Here also Mike received the disappointing news of his A-level results. For a while he was covered in shame; but now, between an 'A' in Spanish and yet more shots of 'B1s' on beer trains (see Chapter 4) there is absolutely no contest!

it very naughty. It fell to me to take it home and secrete it in a pile of underwear. Did I *really* imagine my mother wouldn't find it? My diary, of course, makes no mention of this, observing decorously: 'Went to Menai Bridge and thence to Amlwch on the auto-train. Had some good shots. Then we spent the rest of the day at Menai Bridge. 2 Scots, a Brit, and several Black 5s on passenger. Weather good but cool.' Rather like the Chalford Auto, the Amlwch branch was also a relic of a bygone age and

Above Evening meeting at Harlech: Standard Class 3 2-6-2T No 82006 meets Standard Class 4 4-6-0 No 75002. We had just returned behind the latter from our excursion to Anglesey. *RNI*

Friday 28 August was our Anglesey day. On the outward journey we changed at Pwllheli, where there occurred the disgraceful episode of the Passion Flower Hotel. Mike bought on the station bookstall a paperback of that name, about a group of Sixth Form girls who converted the space under the stage in their school Hall into a bordello, and offered their services to the boys of the academy down the road. By today's standards this more sophisticated version of St Trinian's was extremely mild, but we thought

closed to passenger traffic in 1964, not long after our visit. However, the line continued to be used for freight traffic to and from the Associated Octel plant until 1993.

Three of the four of us travelled home on 29 August via Bala and Ruabon, with a lengthy stay at Bala on the way. The line on from Blaenau Ffestiniog was closed to passengers in 1960 and to freight in 1961; just the branch line train to Bala therefore remained, shuttling to and fro.

Our visit to the Barmouth-Ruabon line was a fortunate finale to our Welsh holiday; by early 1965 the whole of the line west of Llangollen, including the Bala branch, had closed.

Above The Amlwch branch auto-train arrives at Menai Bridge propelled by Ivatt 2-6-2T No 41226 on 28 August 1964. *RNI*

Below Earlier the same day we had had a return journey across the heartland of Ynys Môn on this threatened branch. Here No 41226 waits at Amlwch for her return journey. Sadly there is no sign of the station here at all today. *RNI*

Above 'Black 5' 4-6-0 No 45003 on a parcels train approaches Menai Bridge station from the west on 28 August 1964. *MES*

Below On the same day 'Royal Scot' No 46148 *The Manchester Regiment* (appropriately enough) heads up the 15.30 Holyhead to Manchester as it speeds through Menai Bridge station. (The reflection in the carriage windows picks up the station nameboard.) *MES*

Opposite Before the days of affordable (for teenagers) cine film, how can one record railway movements? Imagine these three shots as an old-fashioned filmstrip.

Top We are at Bala Junction on 29 August 1964 and Mike (with rucksack) watches to ensure uncoupling is carried out by the book.

Middle The loco (Ivatt 2-6-2T No 41241) runs round, with the River Dee in close proximity. (Mike's father once visited the Bala area on a fishing holiday. The signalman then was a keen fellow angler and, on this lightly trafficked line, more time was spent with rod in hand than with lever!)

Bottom Finally, the train is almost ready for departure for Bala. *All RNI*

4
ON THE DOORSTEP:
THE HOME PATCH, 1965-60

The next layer down is the thickest, and in some ways the richest, of all: bits of this complicated site are mixed up with all the others. Our home patch was Burton-on-Trent in Staffordshire, in what is sometimes now, but was never then, called the Heart of England. Home is where the heart is: looking at old photos is always a poignant experience, but for us, sifting through several thousand for this and our previous volume, those of Burton brought the biggest lump to the throat. There we lived right through the time-span of this book, did all our growing-up from short trousers to shaving, and had our education from infant school to A-level. No long journeys were needed to see varied and abundant steam: there it was on the doorstep.

Burton, sited at the junction of routes along and across the valley of the Trent, has a long and distinguished history as a religious and commercial centre, but the two greatest monuments to that history, the abbey church and the mediaeval bridge, are long gone. By the early 19th century, brewing, with water from the local gypsum beds, was already the most important industry, and in the 1960s the breweries were still dominant, both socially and physically; they were the largest employers, and much of their activity took place in the very centre of the town. Thanks to them, Burton was not quite like anywhere else. Modern Burton is cleaner and more orderly, and the town is probably more conscious of its heritage than ever before; but that consciousness has been late in coming, and much of the character has gone.

A major part of that character was due to the railways, whose growth followed and then facilitated the growth of the breweries. (Less happily, their need for a route around the east side of the town was a crucial factor in the replacement of the ancient bridge.) In our day, despite the strike of 1955, which lost much business to the roads, a lot of Burton beer still went by rail, and for its size the town had a lot of railway, including an intricate network of railway corridors around and between the brewery buildings. For us, as young enthusiasts, it was a fascinating place to be: there was always plenty to see and to record.

A meaningful time-line depends on a series of outstanding events. For us at Burton, this is lacking; because we were by the tracks so often, our experiences there have merged into a continuous stream. It's the places that release the memories, as well as the feelings. Some we knew so well that pictures of them bring instant recall and a flood of feeling. Others we visited so rarely that our reaction to the pictures has sometimes been, 'Where on earth was that?' In most cases, a bit of thought brought the answer, but in others it meant tracing a sequence of photographs, consulting maps or

This map is based on Ordnance Survey 1-inch Seventh Series No 120, Burton upon Trent, published 1953, with minor corrections 1960. It shows all the railway lines we knew, and all the stations, open and closed, but even in the 1960s the town was expanding and some recent building is not marked. The blue dots indicate all the photographic locations in Chapter 4, apart from the outlying Potlocks Farm and Stenson Junction in the north-east. *Crown Copyright*

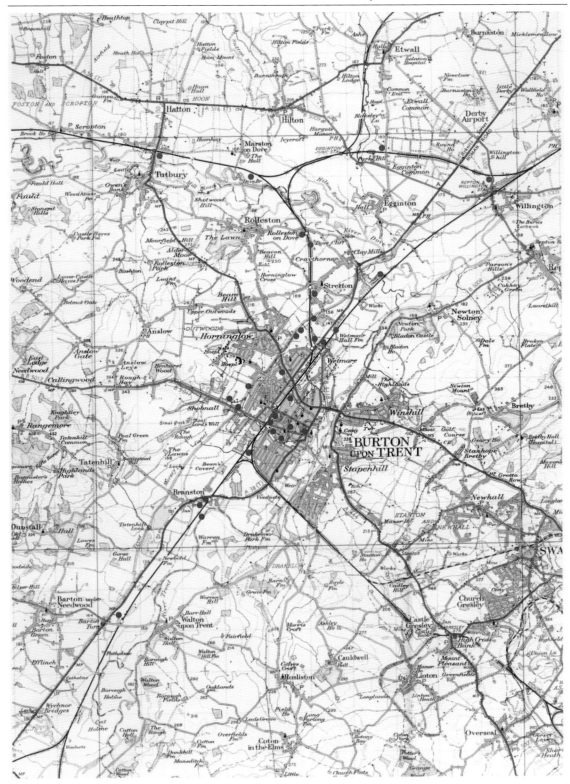

books, or bothering friends. Anyone who has tried to do this kind of thing will know how difficult it is, for views change with astonishing speed; trees have a life of their own, and sometimes it seems as though housing has too, not to mention the ugly spiked palisade fencing and other products of the enterprise referred to below. We've always managed to come up with an answer, but in some cases the burning question remains, 'How did we get that view?' Well, we were lucky enough to be there before the HSE inaugurated its mission to turn the UK into a second DDR.

What follows takes the form of a tour of the area. The outline below is supplemented by the captions. For our own sake as much as the reader's, we've supplied an OS map showing the approximate locations of most of the photographs in this chapter.

The itinerary, which is clockwise, starts and

finishes north of the station at the footbridge known as the Iron Bridges. Since at least the 1880s there has only been a single span there, but an earlier map shows one over the main line and a separate one over the adjacent brewery branch, which doubtless explains why the plural form was and still is always used. This was where I did my earliest spotting, and from here you got the best impression of Burton's railways, its breweries, and their interdependence. And on the horizon to the south was the prominent gable of the MR passenger station, built in 1883 to replace an earlier one nearby.

Like most Victorian stations, Burton's seemed to say that the people who built it were proud of it and of their railway; its 1971 successor, scarcely visible from the Iron Bridges, looks as though BR, brainwashed by Beeching, was ashamed of both. The old structure, of

The Iron Bridges are (or is, see the text) visible in this portrait of Truman's stout little saddle tank and its crew on 24 October 1963. Peckett No 2136 was a mere 10 years old, but by the date of the next photograph it had

been retired; as can be seen in both, the yard had been concreted and shunting could be performed by a road tractor. The loco would have been just out of shot to the right of the 1964 view. *MES*

This was the southward view from the Iron Bridges. In the first picture is 'Black 5' No 45048, heading a freight on the up (Derby-bound) slow line on 20 June 1964.

On 14 May 2011 the substantial station buildings, the bay platform, the abundant sidings and Truman's Black Eagle Brewery have all gone, and little remains apart from the four through tracks, the road bridge,

and, just visible above the trees beyond the houses, the Midland Railway warehouse, together with one of the commercial buildings to its right in Borough Road. (This picture should have featured a Class 67 on a freight, to match the previous shot, instead of the boring 'Voyager', but we were eating our chips out of the wind in the car...) *Both RNI*

Looking north from the station towards the Iron Bridges, in this late-1964 view 'Austerity' No 90279 heads a steel train on the down main line, with the bay platform formerly used by the 'Tutbury Jinny' auto-train on the left and a pre-war LMS BG van at the former horse-and-carriage dock on the right. Apart from the litter, this is a pleasing and orderly scene – everything looks well-planned and well-tended. (Notice the inverted commas round the names of the beers on the façade of Ind Coope's brewery.)

Contrast that with the chaos in this view of an Inter-City 125 in the same position on 14 May 2011. Apparently no one wants to acknowledge ownership of the historic structure, and the rest, from the cones to the invasive buddleia to the modern buildings, is a haphazard mess. *MES/RNI*

Left No doubt the spotters at Burton station on 11 May 1963 were there to see a well-polished Bulleid unrebuilt 'West Country', No 34006 *Bude*, waiting to take over a returning excursion to St Pancras. That they were actually more interested in a grimy 'Jubilee', No 45700 *Amethyst*, passing on a southbound freight, is not so daft as it seems. *Amethyst* had just been transferred to Derby from Newton Heath (Manchester), whose locos tended to elude Burtonians. A Southern 'Pacific' was an interesting curiosity; a rare 'Jube' was to die for. *RNI*

which only fragments remain, had a number of impressive and endearing features, such as the immensely long island platform, with bays at either end; a glazed canopy to match; a veranda that overlooked the platforms; and a fine 1883-dated drinking-fountain. The island interrupts a long straight, so an approaching train on the main line is visible for a couple of miles in either direction, which gave the young enthusiast plenty of time to get steamed up about what the loco might be.

Below Easter Monday excursion 1T19 to Alton Towers pulls into Burton on 30 March 1964 behind Fowler 4F No 44540 and Stanier '5' No 45267. The 4F, additional power for the steep gradients between Leicester and

One of my earliest memories there is of the foggy Christmas Eve (hi, Rudolph!) of 1958, when I copped 'Jubilee' No 45694 *Bellerophon*, very late on the down 'Devonian'. Well satisfied, I left, thus missing one of a class we all dreamed of seeing there, No 72006 *Clan Mackenzie*. I also caught a chill and was in bed over Christmas. Nearly 30 years later, and more than 20 after the end of steam there, I glanced over the bridge on my way to catch a train to work and saw a puff of steam. From

Burton (perhaps via the Swadlincote loop), came off here; we got on, for further photography at Alton. Note the MR lower-quadrant signal. *MES*

some factory, I thought; now, if that had been 25 years ago... As I descended the steps to the platform, a GWR whistle heralded Tyseley's 'Castle' No 5080 *Defiant*, on the way to Derby with its support coach. Tear-jerking or what?

A chapter on Burton would be incomplete without some illustrations of the brewery railways and other industrial railways that criss-crossed the town, and its streets, producing more than 30 level crossings within 2 miles of the town centre. It was only thanks to the intrepid Cliff Shepherd and his excellent *Brewery Railways of Burton on Trent* that we were able to identify some of the more remote locations. Even then it was very difficult to obtain meaningful after-shots to show how

Spot the difference. On Maundy Thursday, 26 March 1964, Standard Class 5 No 73092 enters Burton station with a northbound express, past Burton Station South signal box, Ind Coope's Burton Bottling Store, the bay platform for Leicester and Wolverhampton trains, and the carriage sidings.

The most that can be said of the 'present' view is that it is colourful. Class 37 No 97303 flies jauntily solo through a denuded town- and railscape on 11 March 2011. One item still remaining, visible in the later picture (in matching yellow) but hidden in the earlier, is milepost 11 from Derby, next to the site of the box. *Both RNI*

housing and car parks have transformed industrial Burton.

Our tour then takes us back again to the main line, past our beloved Moor Street Bridge to Branston. This was the southern limit of our frequent visiting; we ventured further, to Barton & Walton or beyond, only if we needed exercise or a change of surroundings.

The return, northward, leg of the itinerary bypasses the town, and in fact follows the route of a line built to do just that, the London & North Western's Dallow branch, which, like so many closed lines, is now partly a trail for walkers and cyclists and partly, guess what, housing. The LNW line left the Midland at Shobnall Junction, and at Stretton Junction

Below 'Somewhere south of New Street, where the best is like the worst': the wheel on the wall on the left was evidently used for target practice by the natives. Rudyard Kipling, to whom apologies for adapting his famous lines, would have had something to say about the election slogan on the right – 'LET'S GO WITH LABOUR' – to somewhere hotter than Suez, perhaps? Kitson 'Dock Tank' No 47000, sent by Derby in late June 1964 to deputise for Burton's Yorkshire Engine Co 0-4-0 diesel No D2859, ploughs through the undergrowth on the curvaceous New Street branch. *RNI*

On 25 June 1964 No 47000, on the same turn, stands near Uxbridge Street level crossing. Note the milepost (from Wellington Street Junction) and the fine array of Midland Railway signals, not to mention Mike, trying to look inconspicuous on the right. The distinctive building in the background is part of Clarence Street Maltings. *RNI*

Left and below Clarence Street then and now. Also on 25 June 1964, No 47000 and friends extract a grain van from the recesses of the Maltings. Mike wishes he'd taken more notice of the flora: Burton used to be famous among botanists for the rich variety of alien plants brought in with grain and timber for the breweries.

The third, present-day view taken on 11 March 2011, should be compared with that of the Horninglow branch on page 100; instead of being demolished to make way for housing and offices, these industrial buildings have been imaginatively adapted as the nucleus of a pleasing development. The gleaming bulbous object is a brewing copper. *RNI/ MES/RNI*

Right The cab of Bass
0-4-0 saddle tank *No 2*
(Neilson Reid No 5760
of 1900) must have been
a congenial working
environment on the
fine morning of 20 July
1963, but what about the
winter? The former Christ
Church shows that engine
and men are about to
cross New Street. *RNI*

Below The south end of
the old Burton station
buildings is seen from
Moor Street crossing,
where much of our youth
was (some would say mis-)
spent. The early afternoon
Derby-Bristol parcels is
leaving behind 'Jubilee' No
45610, which we can just
remember as *Gold Coast*;
the name was changed to
Ghana in 1958. *MES*

In late April 1963 'Black 5' No 44818, on a coal train, passes under what was then the A38 and through Branston station, closed on 22 September 1930.

On 11 March 2011 the bridge is the same but the station has gone. A surprising survival is the boarded crossing to the south, from which this shot was taken of Class 66 No 66084 on a down freight. Network Rail and the train companies wanted a footbridge there, but the locals opposed this on Health & Safety grounds; apparently one is less likely to be killed on the tracks than in one of the opaque claustrophobic erections known as 'Muggers' Alleys'. However, people probably don't wander nonchalantly along the line any more, as Richard did to secure the previous picture. *Both RNI*

Left This is the southward view from the crossing, as 'Jubilee' No 45684 *Jutland* accelerates a Durham-Abergavenny troop train away from Burton at the end of the perfect day (sunny, lots of steam) that had been Saturday 20 June 1964. The backshot shows clearly the first vehicle of the train, an LNER Gresley Brake 3rd, possibly of 1929-39. Would the modern soldier put up with the kind of stock that was so often wheeled out for his predecessors? *RNI*

On 3 October 1964 8F No 48258 drags a load of coal along the slow line south from Branston.

We owe the 'present' view, of kaleidoscopic Class 37 No 37087 *The Keighley & Worth Valley Railway*, with an engineer's train on 11 March 2011, to a tip-off from a group of diesel enthusiasts. Ah well, no doubt they think *we're* mad... *MES/RNI*

Right It was worth using colour for the sake of the signalman's tasteful purple Mini. 8F No 48056, adorned with an irrelevant reporting number, is on a heavy down freight at Barton & Walton, probably in the summer of 1965. *RNI*

joined the North Staffordshire Railway's Burton branch, shared in part by Great Northern trains heading for Derby Friargate and Nottingham. This too is in part a trail; another stretch has suffered another familiar fate and is a suburban road.

On the North Staffs, we often visited Rolleston-on-Dove, where Richard's mother spent her school years, and Tutbury, where our friend Mick Thompson lived, and whose traffic, however meagre, often supplied locos 'rare' to us. These, together with Clay Mills on the Midland main line, marked our usual northern boundary.

A day, or part of one, in the life of 'Jinty' No 47313. On a spring morning in 1963, it sets off from Burton shed and makes its way via Shobnall Junction to the Allsopp's Maltings branch to collect some grain vans. The very rural-looking location of the second photograph resisted identification, but St Paul's Church in the background of the third gave the game away. No 47313 was originally built for the Somerset & Dorset Joint Railway, and was also the last of its class in BR service. *All RNI*

Above The 'ancient' view was taken in February 1964 from the Casey Lane footbridge, which carried the ancient path from Burton town centre to Anslow across the LNWR Dallow branch and the Trent & Mersey Canal. Stanier 2-6-0 No 42972, a rare bird indeed on this branch, shunts some hoppers on what was by then a wagon store but had once been a double-track through route with ample siding provision for adjacent industry.

Below On 11 March 2011 there is no railway at all, and the bridge has been cut back to cross the canal alone. In the 'modern' view, note the narrow boat and the pale the Easter-Island-style objects; these mark the southern end of the Kingfisher Trail, which runs where the railway once did. *MES/RNI*

Left On a hot 25 June 1964, four months after No 42972 was doing its stuff, the Dallow branch was already in course of demolition. 'Jinty' No 47464 has picked up the gang from the end of the line near Stretton Junction and is waiting for them to collect their kit from the hut alongside the Shakespeare Road estate – not yet built when our map was published. *RNI*

'Wiv a ladder and some glasses, / You could see to 'Ackney Marshes, / If it wasn't for the 'ouses in between' (Edgar Bateman, 1894). Beyond No 47464 on its errand of mercy are, left to right, the bridge taking the North Staffordshire's Burton line over the Trent & Mersey Canal, Stretton Junction signal box, and the Pirelli factory.

On 6 November 2010 all that remains from the 1964 view is the top of one Pirelli chimney; if it wasn't for the 'ouses in between you could still see the main factory building. The northern end of the Kingfisher Trail is again appropriately marked. Mock not – just after Richard had taken the after-shot, a kingfisher flew over. *Both RNI*

'B1' No 61070 passes Stretton Junction and is about to cross the Trent & Mersey Canal with an ominously short train of Bass beer tanks on 26 March 1965. A small but annoying question hangs over this picture – which train was it? The ones we usually photographed here were 4N19, the 6.15pm Horninglow-York, and 5E10, the 6.55pm from the same yard to Colwick; we called them 'the Annesley' and 'the Colwick' because those places were where their inward workings started. Mike's notebook suggests the latter, and so does the loco; by this date a 'B1' would have been unusual power for the 6.15. However, the short train and the state of the light fit the earlier train better. Most importantly, No 61070's headlamp code indicates Class 4 (at least 90% vacuum-fitted, as opposed to the 50% of Class 5). Had they 'piped up' the 6.55 and changed the lamps? Hmm… We are looking towards the place on the Dallow branch where the pictures on the previous pages were taken; the closure of that line is confirmed by the removal of the right-hand arm on the signal bracket.

The diesel invasion was nothing to the petrol invasion; as so often, the trackbed where No 61070 once ran has been turned into a road. One of the beneficiaries winks knowingly at the photographer on 6 November 2010. *MES/RNI*

Thompson 'K1' 2-6-0s were unusual visitors on the 6.15 to York. On this occasion in late June 1964 Mike was short of funds and economising on film: 'I shan't take it unless it's a "K1",' he declared. Much to his surprise and everyone else's, it was, so he did, but Richard took two and his backshot is the best of the bunch. The location is Stretton Crossing.

Forty-six years on, the line from Stretton Crossing to Rolleston has become a footpath, known in part as the 'Jinny Trail'. The name commemorates the 'Tutbury Jinny' (variously spelled, but always so pronounced), the auto-train that plied between Burton and Tutbury until 1960. Thanks to Nature, like most such conversions the route is now in a tunnel for most of its length, so the bridge seen in the previous picture would be invisible even if present. In fact, it has been demolished, and the cutting it spanned partly infilled. However, the garage in the right foreground, or at least its successor, remains! *Both RNI*

Above This view was taken beside the footbridge, known to us as Fox Bridge, over the cutting to the south of Rolleston station. An unidentified 9F passes on an up freight, some time in the early spring of 1965. *RNI*

Right 'B1' No 61264, now fortunately preserved, swims through a tank of shade in the cutting with the 6.55pm to Colwick in late June or early July 1964. *MES*

Right No 61210 heads the same train at Rolleston station a few weeks earlier. The buildings are still in reasonable order 15 years after closure on 1 January 1949. Imagine what would happen to them today! *MES*

Above 'B1' No 61264 is seen again, performing a regular manoeuvre at Marston Junction, where the North Staffordshire's Burton branch left its main line towards Derby. On 27 July 1964 the loco is in the course of a freight working to Horninglow Yard, whence it will return with the 6.55pm to Colwick. There are no suitable turning facilities there, so it has left its train at Egginton Junction, and will collect it again when it has turned on the Egginton-Marston-Dove Junction triangle. *RNI*

Below 'Black 5' No 45249 has left its train on the line from Crewe while it does business at Tutbury station on 26 June 1965. *RNI*

Beyond the foregoing is a cluster of 'one-off' sites, on the Friargate line, the NSR's line towards Derby, and the Midland, that again took some identifying – doing that, and visiting some of them, has been part of the fun of writing this book.

Above 'B1' No 61070 again heads 'the Colwick' on 28 June 1965. The location is one we only managed to visit once – a remote and picturesque stretch of line near Potlocks Farm, north of Etwall on the Great Northern 'Friargate line'. *RNI*

Above right and right On the same day we crossed the road at Egginton Goods, east of Egginton Junction on the Derby-Crewe line, just as 8F No 48122 obligingly turned up on a westbound freight.

As the view on 6 November 2010 shows, the crossing house is practically unaltered, but the charming little box for the ground frame has been replaced by something unpleasant. *Both RNI*

Above Perhaps wisely, Richard alleges amnesia here. 8F No 48083 appears to be coming off the line from Sheet Stores at Stenson Junction, but as to why he was there at Easter 1964, or how he came to be in the middle of the down main… *RNI*

Below and above opposite Finding locations 40 years on is not always easy, but the power station and the curve in the track led us quickly to a footpath crossing, still in situ, just west of the Findern road at Willington. Gresley 'A3' No 60051 *Blink Bonny* is in charge of the 'South

Yorkshireman' rail tour from Sowerby Bridge to Crewe on 18 April 1964. *Both RNI*

Below A single-unit railcar is a bit of a comedown from a 'Pacific' and seven coaches. Still, Class 153 No 153321 looks quite sweet as it follows in *Blink Bonny*'s footsteps on 11 November 2010. *RNI*

We return from Clay Mills via Woolley's Bridge, with its good views of the Trent Valley northwards, and Wetmore, where freights with GN and NSR destinations crossed the main line.

Above At Clay Mills you were only 2 miles out of town, but already you were in pleasant countryside, near the confluence of the Dove and the Trent. (It is less pleasant now: the big elms have succumbed to disease, and the gravel workings and the sewage treatment plant are eating their way inexorably towards each other.) 'Jubilee' No 45668 *Madden* heads towards Derby in August 1963 with what is probably the 8.40am Bristol-Sheffield, a lightweight train that was often steam-hauled when 'Peaks' were in short supply. *MES*

Below This northward view from Woolley's Bridge shows Willington Power Station in the far distance and the aforementioned Clay Mills sewage works closer, complete with smoke from the chimney. This is a sight still occasionally to be seen: the steam pumping station has been partly restored to working order by the Claymills Pumping Engines Trust. Smartly turned-out 'Black 5' No 44725, passing with a down freight in July 1964, adds further interest: a former Carlisle (Kingmoor) engine, its large cabside numbers indicate outshopping north of the Border. *MES*

Above LNER 'O1' 2-8-0s were regular visitors with coal from Nottinghamshire and steel from South Yorkshire. No 63872 passes under Wetmore Bridge with a southbound freight on 9 July 1963. The sheds belonged to the citizens of Wetmore Road, who specialised in the keeping of poultry; they still did so until very recently, and perhaps still do. *MES*

Below However, the fires are out as a DMU occupies the same track on 11 March 2011. *RNI*

A brief diversion takes us to the MR Horninglow branch, visible from my bedroom; even in the 1960s it served half a dozen industrial premises in its half-mile course.

Then it is back to the Iron Bridges with its breweries and sidings, the place that, for me, most truly embodied the appeal of the railways on our doorstep.

Above 9F No 92075 has crossed the Midland main line and the A38 at Wetmore and is heading for Stretton Junction and Derby Friargate with the 6.15pm beer train from Horninglow to York in late April or early May 1964. In the background are two well-known Burton landmarks, the Electricity Works on Wetmore Road (right) and the water tower at Waterloo Clump. *MES*

Below You'd wonder where they find the people to fill the flats and houses that have mushroomed and go on mushrooming in place of Burton's industrial buildings. This bland block in Dallow Street, photographed on 8 April 2011, occupies the site of the Renold Chains building, surely one of the most elegant factories ever designed, but heedlessly demolished in 2008. *RNI*

Above The notice prohibits No 47643, as a six-coupled engine, from proceeding – did it or didn't it? The witness saw nothing... *MES*

Below The 'Jinty' shunting the Horninglow branch in November 1964 looks out of place beside this model of modern efficiency; it goes better with the chaos at the premises of the Burton Pure Ice & Cold Storage Co across the way. *MES*

Left Long-time Burton resident 4F No 44599, with its distinctive high-sided tender, is on the down slow line at the Iron Bridges in late autumn 1963; it may be in the course of marshalling its train at Horninglow Bridge sidings, or working a tripper, arrangements for which were apparently fairly relaxed. *RNI*

Below left and below 'Britannias' were never common at Burton, and when Mike, in the garden at home on 3 October 1964, heard the distinctive whistle of the class, he grabbed his camera and jumped on his bike. He reached the Iron Bridges just in time to bag No 70010 *Owen Glendower* in a similar position to No 44599, as it emerged from Horninglow Bridge yard with a fitted freight.

In the recent view, all the buildings have disappeared apart from the bridge, and all the sidings too, but other surviving historic structures are revealed on the left. Class 66 No 66614 is crossing from down slow to main with a freight on 11 March 2011. *MES/RNI*

5
Sit back and wait: the WCML and the WRML, 1965-62

MIKE: Apart from sheds and works (see Chapter 6), the places where spotters were most likely to be found were the main lines, with their frequent long-distance services. Burton didn't quite qualify for this status. There, the freights came from all over, and in fact – especially if you did your spotting at Wetmore and saw the traffic on the so-called Great Northern Bank – a whole day at Burton could be more productive in terms of 'cops' than the West Coast Main Line. But you were unlikely to cop a 'namer', and they were undoubtedly sexier (though that's not a term we'd have used of engines then), hence that part of the Trent Valley was often preferred to ours.

The Western Region Main Line through Birmingham scored high there, too; I always think it says a lot about the GWR that it was prepared to lay out so much brass – literally – on nameplates. And apart from the cops, at Lichfield or Tamworth there was the thrill of seeing big engines travelling fast, or at Hatton, if you could get that far,

of hearing them working hard. This chapter, then, concentrates on two great lines in the West Midlands.

During a day on the West Coast Main Line you would see an awful lot of 'wrecks' (despised machines you'd seen a hundred times before), but there was always a fair chance that one of the green (if grimy) beauties would hail from north of the Border. If it was a 'Semi' (our name for Stanier's 'Coronation' Class) there might be a blue-backed nameplate for confirmation. On the Western, the holiday trains on a summer Saturday came from as far away as the freights at Burton, and you almost always came back with some obscure item from a remote shed to underline in your 'Combine'.

Right This was the West Coast Main Line at Curborough, north of Lichfield, on Cup Final Day, Saturday 7 May 1960. The diesel invasion was well under way, but of 43 trains seen (we were there for another hour or so), 31, or 72%, were steam. All the LMS passenger types were represented, as well as the BR 'Britannias', and we wish we'd had suitable cameras to record those LNW 0-8-0s on their home ground. Cop of the day was of course Polmadie (Glasgow) 'Royal Scot' No 46121 *Highland Light Infantry, City of Glasgow Regiment. RNI*

Right This is part of Mike's 8-hour marathon at Birmingham Snow Hill on 21 July 1962. During that time only three diesels were seen; the two shunters were harmless enough, but 'Western' No D1003 *Western Pioneer* was an unpleasant omen. 'Kings' were still working most of the Paddington trains, and 37 GWR 'namers' were observed. No 'Counties' or 'Manors' on this occasion, however, and rare 'Halls' from Westbury had been seen before, while the Pembroke Dock-Birmingham produced a Worcester 'Grange' rather than the hoped-for South Wales engine. 'Grrrrrrrrr!!!' says the notebook. *RNI*

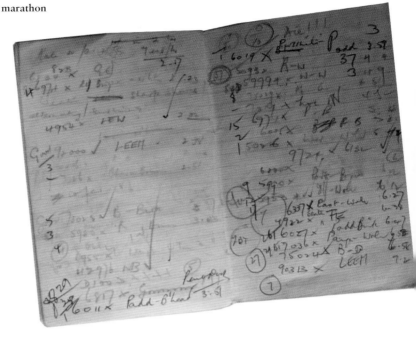

Below Familiarity breeds contempt, and we didn't appreciate just how wonderful a place Burton was for watching trains. These pages show the period 14 November to 4 December 1961.

By this time diesels were in command on most passenger

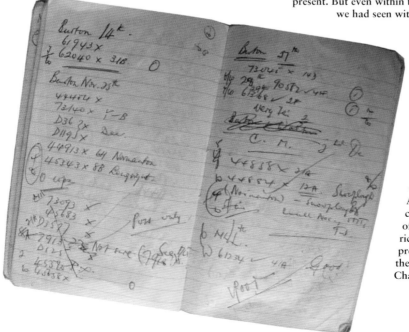

workings (though the 25th saw a 'Standard 5' deputising on our mid-afternoon York-Bristol), but the steam freight scene was remarkably rich. We wrote down only what seemed noteworthy; 'common' stuff was omitted, so the range of types is restricted – for example, 8Fs, 9Fs, 'Jubilees' and 'Jinties' would certainly have been present. But even within the meagre selection recorded we had seen within a month engines from an impressively wide area bounded by York, Retford, Neasden, Woodford, Saltley, Bangor, Warrington and Carlisle – the last, appropriately, with a snowplough. (We thought we'd done even better: against No 62040, really of Retford, I've written 31B (March), and No 61227 of 30F Parkeston Quay would have been a notable cop indeed, but alas it had been transferred to Colwick (Nottingham) – our Ian Allan *Locoshed Books* had not caught up with the dieselisation of East Anglia.) Almost equally rich pickings, from this and the previous year, can be seen in the first and third illustrations to Chapter 6. *RNI*

And we knew the places so well, almost as well as Burton, that watching the decline of steam there was like watching the slow decline of an old friend. Oh, yes – on a good summer Saturday you could kid yourself that it wasn't so bad, but when you compared your records with a year before you couldn't go on pretending. And sure enough, after 1964 at Trent Valley, after 1965 at Snow Hill, there was no more passenger steam.

As with the last chapter, it's hard to trace a meaningful time-line through so many visits, so again the organisation is topographical. In *Steam: The Mystic Harmony* (Silver Link Publishing, 2009) W. Elgar Dickinson has written lyrically about 'favourite spotting spots'. With reference to one such he asks, 'What nicer than sitting in long grass on a sunny slope just watching the passage of clouds against blue skies and smoky steam against cutting sides…?' Indeed, nothing could quite match the luxury of what might be called 'passive spotting', the kind where you just sat there and waited for them to turn up.

And when you'd cycled down there against the prevailing wind the temptation to just take it easy was rather strong, as an increasingly desperate scrabble through negatives and curly old prints has proved. 'What's that?' 'The Maltings at Lichfield.' 'Oh, ah. But where's that?' 'Whittington.' 'How do you know?' 'That's that big tree on the other side of the line.'

Just as Vivaldi wrote the same concerto several hundred times, with only the occasional change of instrument (not fair, I know, but I never did like him), so we have the same picture many times over, with only the occasional change of motive power.

The selection shows what we mean, but we've tried to make the most of what little scenic variety there was, to illustrate most of the locomotive types on offer, and to tell a few stories.

Left Not bad for a Brownie: Richard's trusty Kodak 127 has captured unrebuilt 'Patriot' No 45548 *Lytham St Annes* approaching Lichfield on a down freight. The date is likely to be 1961 or early 1962, certainly before May in the latter year, when it was stored at Rugby pending withdrawal in June. *RNI*

Below BR Standard Class 4 No 75040 takes a short southbound goods through Lichfield Trent Valley High Level and across the West Coast Main Line in April 1963. *RNI*

Above 'Shovelling white steam over her shoulder': W. H. Auden's famous line from *Night Mail* describes a northbound express on the WCML, but this southbound 'Coronation' 'Pacific' ('Semi' to us) is doing the same at Lichfield Trent Valley Low Level, also in April 1963. *RNI*

Left Two more shots on the same day at Trent Valley, as we called it, of trains in the up direction: a 'Black 5' hauling an empty DMU, and a 'Royal Scot' on an express. *Both RNI*

Above The same place later the same year, 31 August 1963, near the end of the summer timetable. Not the best photo, perhaps, but the loco had to be recorded – a 'Clan' through Lichfield was a sight to be seen, and this is No 72009 *Clan Stewart* with what is thought to have been the 12.25pm Blackpool Central-London. The last vehicle of the train, out of shot, was the last 'plum and custard' carriage we ever saw in service. *RNI*

Below Stanier 2-6-0 No 42954 heads a down ballast train on the same day. The numerals on the smokebox numberplate are unusual for the class – which Works used that typeface? The same engine with the same plate can be seen in *Locomotives Illustrated* (22), page 33. *MES*

Above One of the omnipresent 'Whittington trees' (see the text) forms a background for 'Jubilee' No 45554 *Ontario* with a down freight on 1 June 1963. Perhaps looking at the trees prevented us from seeing the pole growing out of the dome... *MES*

Below Another of the trees, and another 'Jubilee', No 45556 *Nova Scotia*, with a London-bound express on Easter Tuesday, 31 March 1964. A strong north-easterly wind helped us reach Whittington on our bikes in record time, but what it did to smoke and steam was nobody's business, and of course we had to get back... *RNI*

Above To avoid the smoke-and-steam problem we crossed the line, without benefit of boards or bridge. We don't know who the mysterious figure was on the up side of the line in the previous shot, but we must have let him get out of the way first! Even so, the driver of 'Semi' No 46256 *Sir William A. Stanier F.R.S.* (how appropriate) is whistling at us – better than stopping the train and calling the police. *RNI*

Below Whittington again, and Cup Final day again, 2 May 1964. 'Britannia' Pacific No 70050 *Firth of Clyde*, with at least 13 coaches, heads 1X17 from Preston to Wembley (17 minutes late at Lichfield) on a day that Roger Newman describes as 'very wet rain (well, it seemed wetter than normal rain) with gloomy skies to match'. *RNI*

Above Another preferred location between Lichfield and Tamworth was Elmhurst Crossing. It too had its fine trees, and in this picture the one nearest the loco seems appropriately to be an elm. Rebuilt 'Patriots', on a par for power with the 'Royal Scots', were a mainstay of the West Coast Main Line. On 20 July 1963 No 45523 *Bangor* heads the 7.55am Blackpool-Crewe, extended on this occasion to Euston. The driver is waving, and not at the photographer – perhaps it was at a family group who were picnicking by the line that day. There had been a notable emergence of the handsome red-and-blue-black cinnabar moth, which breeds on the ragwort that flourished there, and which the little girl of the party was gleefully pursuing. 'Don't encourage them, darling,' said her mother. How do you…? *MES*

Below Notice the holder for the single-line tablet on Edge Hill (Liverpool) 'Black 5' No 45466, indicating its former residence at Carlisle (Kingmoor). It has a tough assignment with the down 'Lakes Express', approaching Elmhurst on 11 July 1964. What had been a regular 'Semi' turn in 1963 (see *Moved by Steam*, page 69) was now booked for nothing bigger than this. Mike's notebook also records some depressing figures for WCML steam haulage, to compare with the 72% in 1960 at the beginning of this chapter: 1962, 50%; 1963, 31.5; 1964, 18.2. *MES*

Logs: Leamington Spa to Birmingham Snow Hill							
(1) 09.23 Bournemouth-Manchester and Liverpool, 3 July 1965.							
Loco: 6976. Load: 12.							
(2) 8.45am Margate and 9.30am Ramsgate to Wolverhampton, 7 September 1963.							
Loco: 6845. Load: 12.							
		(1)			(2)		
miles		sched	actual	mph	sched	actual	mph
0.00	LEAMINGTON SPA	0	0.00	-	0	0.00	-
1.95	Warwick		4.15	39		3.55	
6.10	Hatton		11.10	38		11.20	
	mp 114¾			53			54
10.30	Lapworth		16.49	44*		16.55	56
12.85	Knowle & Dorridge		20.07	48		19.40	50
16.25	SOLIHULL		24.02	55		23.15	64**
20.00	Tyseley		28.38	44*		26.55	66***
22.00	Bordesley		31.13	49		28.55	
23.30	SNOW HILL	35	33.27	-		30.50	-
* Engine eased							
** Speed at Olton							
*** Speed at Acocks Green							

Below **This page from the 1964 Summer Saturday timetable for the WR Main Line through Birmingham shows the range and volume of traffic, much of it to and from holiday resorts, on this important inter-city and cross-country route. The typeface and layout are still those of a Western Region publication, but in fact this was now the London Midland. Three years on, expresses would have ceased to serve Snow Hill, and the station would close altogether in 1972.**
RNI

On 'the Western in the Midlands' there was a much greater variety of locations, from rural Warwickshire through metropolitan Birmingham to the Black Country. On two trips to Leamington we had ex-GW steam both ways from Birmingham Snow Hill. One of them, behind a 'Modified Hall', is described in *Moved by Steam*, but without a log; we make up for that here, and give the other, behind a 'Grange', for comparison. (It's a matter for regret that we have no logs at all of steam runs on the West Coast Main Line.)

With hindsight – and more disposable income – we should have spent more time still on this splendid line, but taken all together what follows gives some idea of the interest, especially the ex-GWR interest, still remaining there in the mid-1960s, as does a page from the public timetable for Summer 1964.

Above The larger Great Western passenger types were barred from large areas of the Southern Region. To avoid changing engines, some Summer Saturday trains from the West Midlands to the Kent and Sussex coasts via Reading were worked through by 'Manors' or '4300' Class 'Moguls'. In *The Day of the Holiday Express* Richard Woodley describes some spirited performances on these trains. No 7818 *Granville Manor* looks set for one such as it leaves Leamington Spa with the 10.30am Birmingham Snow Hill-Hastings on 7 September 1963. *MES*

Below Later the same day 9F 2-10-0 No 92001 leads an up freight on the through road at Leamington. The buildings and background are virtually unaltered in 2011. *MES*

The next three pictures show holiday trains between Hatton and Lapworth on Saturday 1 August 1964. In the first, 'Grange' No 6803 *Bucklebury Grange* breasts the summit of Hatton Bank at Hatton North Junction with possibly the 1.11pm Portsmouth Harbour-Wolverhampton; the chord to Stratford lies beyond. This engine had a particularly good reputation and we describe a run behind it in *Moved by Steam*.

When a colleague described a 'Castle' as 'an elegant engine', his girlfriend expressed scorn and incredulity. Such prejudice! Such poor taste! (Quite – hers, of course.) No 7023 *Penrice Castle* heads south towards Hatton with 1O26, the 10.42am Wolverhampton-Ramsgate.

Northbound at the same location, 'Modified Hall' No 7917 *North Aston Hall* has 1M10, the 10.10am Poole-Birkenhead (no Health & Safety issues then!). *All RNI*

Right An aggressive interloper from the LMS: 'Jubilee' No 45703 *Thunderer* thunders through Knowle & Dorridge with a Preston-Oxford football special on 29 February 1964. *MES*

Below A year later the 'Castles' had almost gone, but 'Granges' and 'Halls' could still be seen and photographed at the same spot. On 31 July 1965 No 6849 *Walton Grange*, with the southbound relief 'Pines Express', displays the pleasing lines of the class and the diagnostic feature of a kinked running plate. *MES*

Bentley Heath, between Dorridge and Widney Manor, was perhaps the classic location for 'passive spotting' on the WR Main Line. Four tracks, a low cutting, a slight curve, excellent views – sit back and enjoy. On 19 June 1965 the up and down reliefs to the 'Pines' were both 'Hall'-hauled, by Nos 5971 *Merevale Hall* and 6930 *Aldersey Hall* respectively. Both look to be on their last legs; asking them to cope with 400 tons plus was a bit optimistic, and they were about 35 and 25 minutes late. Alas! *Both MES*

These next four views show the much beloved and much lamented 'old' Snow Hill. In the first, 'Manor' No 7823 *Hook Norton Manor* has arrived with the 8.35am from Barmouth on 13 July 1963. Other days, other ways… *MES*

The late, great R. C. Riley contrasted the 'compact and tidy' Snow Hill with the 'vast and untidy conglomeration of lines' at New Street. The pleasing layout of the GW station is evident as No 6803 *Bucklebury Grange* (again) stands at Platform 5 with the 11.22am Newquay-Wolverhampton on 18 July 1964. *MES*

Freight traffic avoided New Street almost completely; one of the pleasures of Snow Hill was a down tripper emerging smokily from the tunnel and trundling along the through road, like this one behind a '5600' Class 0-6-2T on 3 July 1965. *MES*

Above Stanley Baldwin, three times Prime Minister, was a West Midland man. In 1964 Oxley's best 'Castle' was probably No 5063 *Earl Baldwin*. It was a regular on the demanding West of England services, and is seen here with the 11.05am Ilfracombe-Wolverhampton on 1 August. *RNI*

Below This is the Saturday Ilfracombe-Wolverhampton again, entering West Bromwich on 18 July 1964 behind Oxley's No 5056 *Earl of Powis*. The last vehicle of the train was in the increasingly rare chocolate-and-cream livery. *MES*

6
THERE FOR THE TAKING: MORE COPS FOR YOUR MONEY, 1963-61

MIKE: In the early 1960s a young man's fancy turned not to thoughts of love, or even to sex, booze and computer games, but to locomotives, and our steamiest scenarios featured the line upon line of these to be found at an important shed (Motive Power Depot or MPD if you wanted to be posh) or works. To see, or more importantly to 'cop', the greatest number of numbers in a day, that was where you had to be; and when money was tight, the number of cops per trip out was a real consideration.

There was nothing to equal the sheer thrill of approaching a big shed – there they all were, yours for the taking – or the sustained, pent-up excitement of making your way up and down those lines, straining at the leash (you couldn't go too fast or you wrote things down wrong), and wondering what treasure lay round the next corner.

It was best to go to a depot on a Sunday, of course: there were fewer trains, hence more engines idle on shed. Another advantage of a Sunday was that most of the inhabitants were likely to be natives, home to roost for the weekend, so if you needed a particular loco you could (with luck) track it to its lair.

The same kind of hunting expedition was sometimes

Top right The calculation at the top of this page from Mike's notebook shows the price per cop of two trips during October half-term, 1961. The cost (adult) to Crewe was evidently 5s 2d, to Wolverhampton 4s 1d. The total number of cops was 111, which works out at exactly 1 penny per cop. We suspect a bit of creative accounting… *RNI*

Above This impressively neat (for Mike) list is from his Posh Record Book, and shows what a lot of Ardsley's and Copley Hill's allocations were at home to visitors on Sunday 22 May 1960. *RNI*

Above An enticing panorama at Motherwell MPD on 25 August 1963, with Standard Class 5 No 73005 prominent. *MES*

Below The Scottish 'WD' 2-10-0s really *did* look bigger than the 2-8-0s. A Saltley driver's description of a 9F, quoted by Terry Essery, might well apply to them: 'Bloody great thing, all boiler and wheels'. No 90756, at Motherwell MPD on the same day, was the first of the class we'd seen. *MES*

necessary for whole classes. OK, so the S&D 2-8-0s visited Derby Works – you might even see one at Burton en route – but the 'Austerity' 2-10-0s stayed in Scotland for overhaul and rarely crossed the Border for any other purpose, and some other types never left the safety of Kent or South Wales (see below). A large depot a long way away gave you both quantity and quality, i.e. rarity.

Although the prime purpose was to fill your notebook with numbers, another special thing about a shed visit was its intimacy; this was the engines' home, and you were privileged to see something of the way they lived – the regular routines of lighting-up, preparation, boiler washouts, routine maintenance and minor repairs. Not to mention the way their minders lived; you couldn't fail to notice the dirt and discomfort, the cold and the clutter, the harsh working conditions of shed staff and footplate men. We cosseted kids didn't know we were

Below The 'Spamcans' were perhaps the most impressive locos of all from ground level. Whales? Icebergs? Airships? 'Battle of Britain' No 34057 *Biggin Hill* suggests any or all of these at Salisbury on 5 September 1962. *RNI*

born, and it was salutary for us to be there, literally on the ground; the beasts towered above you, and you saw the railway in a truer perspective than ever you could from a station platform.

As time went on, though, this privileged insight involved a painful irony, for here, at the living heart of the steam railway, you were most sharply aware of its approaching death. Even in this deep layer of our 'dig', the soil shows signs of pollution by diesel oil. Many, perhaps the majority, of the steam locos we saw on our shed visits would never turn a wheel for money again, and those that still might looked more and more dirty and run down. Would that we'd started 'serious' photography six months earlier, so as to have had, say, a record of the MR 2Fs in steam that cost us an exhausting bike-ride to Coalville on 17 August 1962, instead of the permanently dead one pictured on page 127!

The purely economic aspect of our hobby applied to works as well as sheds; on my first visit to Crewe in 1959 I notched up 61 cops; at Swindon in 1962, 56. But the make-up of those numbers, at sheds and works, was quite

different, in fact opposite: at a shed, especially on a Sunday, you got – hopefully – what you wanted from there; at a works, you hoped for things from all over. And if at a shed you saw an engine at home, here, even more intimately, you saw it in hospital.

At a shed, as we've just said, the last days of steam brought home to us the contrast between dead and alive. At a works, that opposition had always been there: some locos were there to be overhauled, repainted and turned out to earn their keep for another five years or so, but for others it was literally the chop. The contrast was even more poignant, some in spanking trim, others from whom it was kinder to avert one's gaze.

Visits to sheds and works became noticeably fewer after we stopped taking numbers in 1963.

Right Another page from the Posh Record Book displays the exciting variety of types and shed-codes at Crewe Works on 29 February 1960. *RNI*

Below GW 'Castle' No 7000 *Viscount Portal* undergoes treatment at Wolverhampton Works on 24 March 1963. *RNI*

	44144	2 m	✓	42~~~~	
✓	48250	3A		45529*	5A
	45505*	9A		42564	8A ✓
✓	44780	8F	✓	49373	~~8A~~ 3A
✓	48726	3D		45240	5A
	52312	CW		44743	27A ✓
	70052*	66A	✓	92073	16D ✓
	46511	89A	✓	41231	84K ✓
✓	42881	12A	✓	45371	12B
	49404	8A	✓	78017	12D ✓ ✓
	45639*	55A		45058	3D ✓
	45038	5B		44920	21A
✓	D5061	31B		45539*	9A
✓	49094	1E	✓	42435	27C ✓
✓	42278	21H	✓	44800	6B ✓
	90312	86C	✓	45555*	12B
✓	45209	24B	✓	45542*	24K ✓

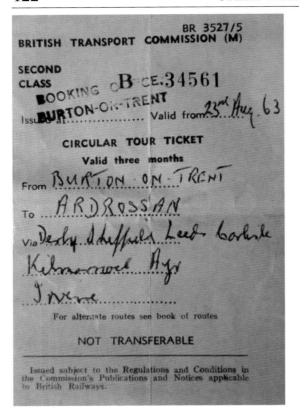

BR 3527/5

BRITISH TRANSPORT COMMISSION (M)

SECOND
CLASS

BOOKING OB CE.34561

Issued at BURTON-ON-TRENT

Valid from 23rd Aug. 63

CIRCULAR TOUR TICKET

Valid three months

From BURTON ON-TRENT

To ARDROSSAN

Via Derby Sheffield Leeds Carlisle
Kilmarnock Ayr
Irvine

For alternate routes see book of routes

NOT TRANSFERABLE

Issued subject to the Regulations and Conditions in
the Commission's Publications and Notices applicable
to British Railways.

In the sequence that follows, from that year to 1961, we've tried to illustrate some of what we've just described, and a few more things as well. In *Moved by Steam* we told the story of our shed-bashing tours of Southern England and Scotland in 1963. That was the end of such tours for us; having given up number-taking on our return from Scotland, there wasn't the same urge. Already by that time the 'dead-and-alive' aspect was very noticeable, as the next few pictures show; but others were noticing it

Left Any ticket from Burton-on-Trent to Ardrossan must be a fairly uncommon item, but as part of a circular tour, extremely so – though at least two others were issued! It is a treasured memento of the gruelling first (overnight) leg of our Scottish shed-bash in August 1963. *RNI*

Below 'The Wee Black Yins': the name shows the affection in which the LMS 2Ps were held by Glasgow & South Western men. One Stranraer driver exclaimed to David L. Smith, 'Oh man, man, they fairly like them! Gey near tak' them tae their bed wi' them!' No 40670 'got the reputation of a very fast engine' at Corkerhill (Glasgow) in the 1930s; it ended its days as station pilot at Dumfries, where it was active until May 1962. Withdrawn as the last of the class at the end of the year, it could still be seen there on 24 August 1963. *RNI*

Above The *Railway Observer* for November 1963 speculated that the surviving ex-Caledonian locomotives would 'finish their days on the G.&S.W. – a rather ironic situation considering the pre-Grouping relations of the two companies'. At Ardrossan on 24 August we found several Caley 0-6-0s, including 'Standard Goods' (or 'Jumbo') Class 2F No 57336 and '812' Class 3F No 57566. No 57336 was still at work in September; No 57566 had recently been withdrawn, but was happily destined for preservation. It is currently at the Strathspey Railway, in blue livery as Caledonian Railway No 828. *RNI*

Below The victor and the not yet vanquished: 'A1' 'Pacific' No 60142 *Edward Fletcher* looks in fine form at Haymarket MPD on 26 August 1963, but three years later the class was extinct and thenceforward no 'A1' was seen on British metals until new-build *Tornado* came along. Richard has shown his contempt for the usurping 'Deltic' by cutting off part of its nose. *RNI*

Above In comparison, 'D49' No 62712 *Morayshire*, already withdrawn and with nameplates and connecting-rods removed, looks most forlorn, but in fact this late example of a 4-4-0 was stored awaiting preservation when we saw it at Dalry Road MPD on 26 August 1963. A stencilled (?) '49' can be made out on the buffer-beam *(enlargement right)*. MES

Below 'Number off from the left...': 'N' 2-6-0s Nos 31867 and 31868 await the firing-squad at Redhill MPD on 13 August 1963. MES

too, and we also saw the first stirrings of the preservation movement.

Earlier the same year I went to Swindon Works, Richard to Crewe, and both of us to Derby, our last visits to those great institutions. As in a hospital, sickness, health, treatment, recovery, death and even resurrection could be found here side by side.

Right A price increase of a shilling was no joke in 1963, but as the accompanying picture shows it was worth it, especially with 'H' power in both directions between Three Bridges and East Grinstead. *RNI*

Above Remarkably, at the time of our visit, some services from Tunbridge Wells and Three Bridges were still operated by motor trains with push-and-pull-fitted 0-4-4 tanks of antique design. Wainwright SEC Class 'H' No 31263, a design introduced in 1904, was in steam at Tunbridge Wells MPD on 13 August 1963. *RNI*

Right Sacrilege! The last of the Great Western 'Kings' had been withdrawn only a couple of months before, but No 6011 *King James I* has already been deprived of its tender (though not its nameplates and cabside numberplates), and is obviously due for early dismemberment. The 'Kings' were introduced in 1927, and on 19 April 1963, when this picture was taken at Swindon Works, there must have been many men still employed there who had helped to build them. *MES*

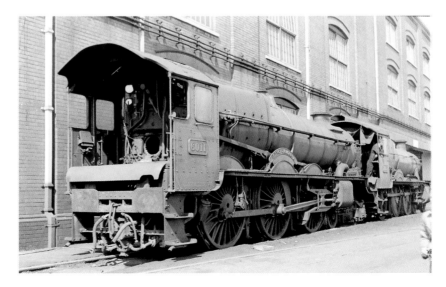

In retrospect, the staff of British Railways were extraordinarily tolerant to us young spotters, and they treated us like adults, unlike some of their successors, whose political masters force them to treat adults like children. Mr D. Wright, of the North Eastern Region at York, was known not only for the turquoise ink of his signature on permits to visit MPDs, but also for his readiness to issue them. I had asked for permission to visit Holbeck (55A) and Neville Hill (55H) 'for purposes of photography' (you had to give a respectable

Left On 24 March 1963 Richard joined at Burton a Derbyshire Railway Society special, 'Clan'-hauled, to Crewe Works via Tyseley and Wolverhampton. All participants were given an Edmondson-style individual permit for Crewe Works. Alert readers will spot that the date is wrong; the tour had, in fact, been postponed from its original date of 27 January. *RNI*

Above The curious style of permit is perhaps explained by the fact that the train actually ran into the Works yard at Crewe, where it is being manoeuvred by 'Jinty' No 47482, complete with Class 'A' headlamps! *RNI*

Left Certain of the BR Class 2 2-6-2 tanks, which we had known on Burton's beloved 'Tutbury Jinny' service in the 1950s, ended their days as Crewe Works shunters. Behind No 84022 is an LMS 4F, of which two survived here in the same capacity until late 1966 and were the last of the class. *RNI*

Above Local Kitson 'Dock Tank' No 47000 has just been outshopped at Derby Works on 26 February 1963. It looks a lot smarter than it did when it explored the back streets of Burton in June 1964 (see Chapter 4). *RNI*

Below No coat of paint for veteran MR 2F 0-6-0 No 58138, on the scrapline at Derby on the same day. It had been one of the small remnant of the class retained to work through Glenfield Tunnel on the Leicester West Bridge branch, which nothing else of appropriate power would fit. We had seen it at Coalville only six months before. *RNI*

reason) on the evening of 2 March 1963, after a school visit to Leeds University. Mr Wright's response suggested politely that the evening of 2 March 1963 might not be the best time for photography. True, I replied, but we'd still like to go. Back came the permits, complete with turquoise signature.

The last chapter of this book features some of our earliest, pre-35mm, photographic attempts, but a few must find a place here.

There has to be something from our South Wales tour in 1962, a milestone for me as I'd never before spent nights away from home without my parents or Richard's. And of course Burton shed has to get a look-in, and the class of which it was the sole, though apparently not the proud, owner.

Moved by Steam relates how Mick Thompson passed on to us the running of his brainchild, the "Wanderers" Railfans' Club.

Above **Mr Wright** (see the text) did try to tell us! The darkest area is all that can be seen of 'J39' 0-6-0 No 64922, withdrawn together with the rest of the class the previous year, at Leeds Neville Hill MPD on 2 March 1963. (Note the NER tender...) There was plenty of interest there for the spotter, including former Holbeck 'Royal Scots' (also withdrawn), and 'A3s', but as to photography – well, how Wright he was! *MES*

Opposite upper Two classes based entirely in South Wales were the '4200' 2-8-0 tanks and the '67XX' series of '5700' pannier tanks, which had steam brakes only and were confined to shunting work. Nos 4254 and 6763 were photographed at Newport (Pill) MPD on August 1962. The veteran vehicle on the left is a GWR Dean clerestory bogie coach of the period 1892-1905. These carriages represented a leap forward for the Great Western, whose earlier passenger stock, antiquated in design, had a poor reputation. *RNI*

Opposite lower Five LMS Hughes-Fowler 2-6-0s were experimentally fitted with rotary valve gear, first the Lentz and later (under BR) the Reidinger version. The 'Reidinger Crabs' were concentrated at Burton, and were used on beer trains to London, Bristol and elsewhere, but like most mavericks were apparently more trouble to maintain than the standard type. Both sorts were supplanted there by 'Jubilees' from late 1961, and the Reidinger engines were withdrawn not long after. The variant was identified visually by the slender rotary shaft that led from the cylinder to the middle driving wheel, where it connected with the big end. No 42825 was in store when it was photographed on the depot, probably in early 1962. The 3F to the right is No 43793, one of the fast-diminishing MR Deeley batch of 1906. *MES*

My personal record for cops on a shed, 124 at Stratford, East London (30A), was on a WRC tour, on 17 April 1961. A bit of a cheat, this, as some were diesels, but we would never see its like again, and the London visit was perhaps the climax of Mick's career as a tour organiser. The last trip under his aegis was to the Manchester area on 16 July 1961.

Above The eponymous doyen of the 'Britannia' Class was the star among 124 cops for Mike at its home depot of Stratford on 17 April 1961. The tank engine in the left background is thought to be a 'J69' 0-6-0, a class introduced nearly 50 years before the 'Brits'. *RNI*

Below A sight for the connoisseur at Springs Branch MPD, Wigan, on 16 July 1961 was the two surviving Great Central 'J10' 0-6-0s, long stored there and withdrawn the following month. No 65157 was actually built for the Manchester, Sheffield & Lincolnshire Railway, and was that company's last surviving loco. *MES*

Above An interesting mixture at Birkenhead MPD on 27 April 1962, with 'Modified Hall' No 6972 *Beningbrough Hall* on the extreme left an 8F, Stanier 2-6-0 No 42970, and 'Jubilee' No 45674 *Duncan. RNI*

Right An interim list of participants on our maiden expedition to the Liverpool district on 27 April 1962, not all of whom were actually able to attend. We are still in touch with several of these people; some others, sadly, have passed on. *RNI*

Our first was to Liverpool on 27 April 1962. Help! Would enough people sign up? Would they all come? Could we find the way, and could we pay the coach company? All was well: the experience has stood us in good stead ever since, and we still have not only the street map of Liverpool bought for the occasion but also a list of participants, and some quite decent pictures from our good old Kodak Brownie 127s.

We end this chapter with a more personal memory of Mick T.. Soon after Christmas 1959 he ran a trip to Leicester and Derby, by train with a Circular Tour Ticket. I couldn't go, as I was ill, and I greatly envied those, including Richard, who had a run from Leicester to Derby behind a 'Royal Scot' (I've still not done that line with steam). On Derby shed they saw another member of the class, No 46123 *Royal Irish Fusilier*, and great was the rejoicing, for it was Mick's Last Scot.

Above **Mick's Last Scot. No 46123** *Royal Irish Fusilier*, **recently transferred to Kentish Town depot, stands on one of the turntable roads at Derby MPD around New Year 1960.** *RNI*

EPILOGUE: THOSE WERE THE DAYS

RICHARD: At last and lowest we come to real buried treasure – memories almost (but not quite) unsullied by the prospect of the end of steam. Unfortunately, our photographs match them neither in quantity nor quality. However, thanks to the wonders of modern technology, there is something to show.

One of my treasured possessions is an old-fashioned Photo Album, helpfully embossed with the words 'Photo Album' for those of us who are beginning to forget what's what, which contains around 16 'sugar paper' pages. Each page has a print and these represent my earliest railway photographs. Some may even have been taken, not with the Brownie 127, which was my second camera, but with a Box Brownie. As recounted elsewhere, we both received 35mm cameras at Christmas 1962, so all the Brownie 127 shots come from an earlier date. In my case, I know I must have started taking the occasional picture as early as 1957, as one such picture (from the album) can be dated accurately, and appeared in *Moved by Steam*.

For my contribution to this, the deepest stratum of our digging back, I have chosen shots from each of the four Regions of BR as we knew it, doing my best not to duplicate Mike's locomotives and locations. We shall be in trouble with SR fans, because the Southern has only one photo in this chapter. It simply illustrates our geographical limitations at this stage of our lives.

Below 'Donald, where's yer trewsers?' Are we alone in thinking the 'Q1s' were naked below the waist? They may have been made in times of austerity, but there are limits... On 1 September 1962 No 33012 rounds the curve into Bournemouth Central with a down freight, past a nostalgic reminder of the days when homing pigeons were released from railway stations. *RNI*

There was a real elegance about the 'County' Class. However, No 1027 *County of Stafford* had an extra appeal for Staffordshire lads: not just the name, but also its allocation to distant Neyland. It has arrived at Carmarthen on 29 August 1962 with what we believe is the train from West Wales, on which we subsequently travelled to Swansea behind a brace of 'Castles'. *RNI*

'Hall' No 4909 *Blakesley Hall* battles with the snow and a long westbound freight at Swindon on 2 January 1962. *RNI*

This view of Lichfield Trent Valley in the high summer of 1961 (?) was taken – nervously – much too early, but it focuses attention on the typical crowd of short-trousered youngsters, and conveys the atmosphere of excitement and anticipation that abounded there in those far-off days. By the far fence is what would now be called a 'responsible adult' – in human language, a father – carrying a very young spotter indeed. The 'Royal Scot', No 46144 *Honourable Artillery Company*, and its express are on the up through line, universally known as the 'clanger', allegedly because of the 'clang' of the balance weight as the tall signal, visible above the bridge, was returned. *RNI*

One of the fascinating experiences of having published *Moved by Steam* – and given illustrated talks about it and our 'railway years' – has been the reaction of our readers to the memories we have shared. Most (we are glad to report) have been positive, but, living in Bedford and serving the county through which run both the Midland and Great Northern main lines, I find myself having to respond to the remark that 'there's not much in it on the East Coast line'. This is a charge that will be levelled against the present volume too. Again, there is a simple answer – we rarely went there.

However, we have a tiny consolation prize for all GN lovers. This is Peterborough very early in the 1960s. Not only is it an 'A4' 'Pacific', and not only is it hauling one of the famous named trains, 'The Elizabethan', but it is the world record-holder No 60022 *Mallard*. The joy of this young railfan was boundless.

An iconic, nay, *the* iconic, locomotive and train (see the text) passes Peterborough en route for Edinburgh in the earliest 1960s. *RNI*

On this or another of our rare visits to the ECML, and in one of those mid-afternoon lulls that seemed to afflict all main lines, I was hopping around on new telegraph poles laid horizontally on a frame by the trackside. One rolled and my leg slipped off into the gap and I fell through. My left wrist took my weight as I broke my fall between the logs. My fall was broken, but so was my fifth metacarpal bone. A pot was needed and had to be in place for six weeks. During this time I went for a prearranged stay with my Great Uncle Charles at Sampford Arundel, near Wellington in Somerset. While he couldn't understand why I wanted a day in Exeter watching trains rather than trying to keep up with him on walks in the countryside, I did manage to get a day there.

We have subtitled this volume 'Trains in retrospect, 1967-60'. It seems appropriate that, as most of my last shots of steam are of 'Halls' in Oxford, I should close with my earliest shot of a (Modified) 'Hall' at Exeter in 1960.

•

MIKE: One of *my* treasured possessions is a collapsing shoebox of mid-1960s vintage inscribed 'PHOTOGRAPHIC EQUIPMENT: SUCH AS IT BE'. Until I extracted them for the present project, it included two groups of Brownie 127 prints of various sizes, with no accompanying negatives. For 50 years, more or less, they have coped with the routine hazards of sharing my life. They have also survived two less predictable disasters, from which each was saved by a miracle.

At some time (I prefer not to guess when), I looked at the first group, noticed their defects of composition, and thought they might look better chopped into pieces and reassembled as what I called a 'RAILWAY MOSAIC'. Courtesy of Photoshop Elements 8, some of them have been restored to something like what they were.

I treated the second group with greater respect, and they were in fact considered for

Above This 'Brownie 127' shot represents the lowest stratum of our material 'Out West'. In the summer of 1960 'Modified Hall' 4-6-0 No 7901 *Dodington Hall* awaits departure from Exeter St David's. Two '1400' Class 0-4-2Ts can be glimpsed simmering gently next to a 'Prairie' tank on Exeter MPD. *RNI*

possible publication in one of Mike (Mick) Thompson's articles (see Chapter 1). But at some time (again I prefer not to guess when, or indeed why) I must have been looking at them in bed. Beside the bed, in my house in Cambridge, was a shelf with a pile of old *Punch* magazines, kept there as a soporific. The photographs, in an original envelope from Mick T., went on top of this pile, and another similar pile went on top of them. The miracle this time was that in removing the magazines for disposal prior to a change of career and locale, I happened to separate them into the two original piles, with the envelope between them. If I hadn't, the photographs would have gone to the tip.

The items thus saved for posterity include no masterpieces, but I'm glad to have them back, for they show trains in places that mean a lot to me, and some of the places are classic locations, immortalised by the great names in railway photography. Every enthusiast will have wanted to have a go at pictures there; my efforts are piffling in comparison, but Shakespeare, as usual, put it best: they are 'a poor thing, but mine own'. That adds to their value for me, and they evoke many memories, further back.

In 1961, the family holiday was at Barmouth, on the Cambrian Coast line. I spent a good part of that week standing beside the line in Barmouth, brooding, in suitably grey Welsh weather, not only on trains but also on the daughter of the house we were boarding in; I've had a thing about Welsh women ever since.

Brighter weather on the Thursday took me out of myself on a trip to Aberystwyth. We (that's my parents and me, of course, not HER and me) changed at Dovey Junction, where we watched the coupling-up of the Pwllheli and Aberystwyth portions of the 'Cambrian Coast Express', which went off to Shrewsbury behind Machynlleth's pride and joy at the time, No 7803 *Barcote Manor*.

Our own trips along the undulating line through Ynyslas and Borth were also 'Manor'-hauled, by Nos 7800 *Torquay Manor* and 7815 *Fritwell Manor*; with their gleaming brass and copper and their trenchant exhausts, they looked and sounded as if they really meant business, unlike the dirty dilatory Stanier products, their hoarse beat seeming to betoken permanent poor health, that I was used to at home. (Of course, I'll make an exception for the 'Jubilees'.)

The year before, we'd been further away

Left Collett 0-6-0 No 2204 leaves Barmouth Bridge and enters the cutting at the approach to the station with a down freight on 14 August 1961. When Richard took the shots in Chapter 3, three years later, very few of these locos remained on the Cambrian system; we saw only one in steam during our stay in the area. *MES*

Below The 'Cambrian Coast Express' was still 'Manor'-hauled as late as 1965, but under London Midland rule the men at Aberystwyth seemed no longer to take quite the pride in them that they had under the Western. The most cosseted of all, No 7803 *Barcote Manor*, waits at Dovey Junction with the up train on 17 August 1961. Mike's trip to Aberystwyth that day was evidently a success: the term FIN! (a Goon expression signifying elation – the opposite was SPON!) occurs seven times on the relevant page of his notebook, whose concluding words are '19 cops in day. Exquisite! MES'. *MES*

Left The 'Manor' beside the sea wall at Teignmouth on what appears to be an engineering train is almost certainly No 7808 *Cookham Manor*, and the date Sunday 14 August 1960. *MES*

Left Even Richard's skill with Photoshop cannot quite redeem this rather sketchy impression of an evening beer train at Stretton Crossing, circa 1960. Would that it looked more like Michael Mensing's beautiful study on the back cover of Mark Higginson's *The Friargate Line*! But it is Mike's only shot of a Gresley 'K3' in action, and enshrines a precious memory of these lovely locos, a mainstay of those services at that time. *MES*

Left The fireman of Bristol Barrow Road's unrebuilt 'Patriot' No 45504 *Royal Signals* looks less than happy as it waits at Burton with the northbound 'Devonian', again around 1960. The crew would have been from the same depot, and the men there were said not to think much of the three members of the class they acquired in late 1958. Is the presence of a 'Black 5' as pilot simply due to the load, or was the 'Pate', despite its smart appearance, playing up that day? The accompanying log shows that it could perform well enough when it chose. *MES*

for longer, and the venue must have been my choice: Teignmouth, in Glorious Devon, glorious for me because our accommodation was two minutes from the GW main line. Although the *Torrey Canyon* had yet to pollute the coastal waters of the West, a tide of diesel oil was starting to invade the ultra-famous piece of railway along the sea wall, with 'Warships' already in charge of the 'Cornish Riviera Express' and suchlike. But the fortnight added 440 numbers to my collection, only 58 of them diesel, and thanks to the profligate GWR policy I praised in Chapter 5, 200 of the steam cops were named. Wow. I was too busy writing them down to photograph more than a tiny number of them, but one is included, another 'Manor', in a place where they were more rarely seen.

Of course we must include some Burton pictures. My one shot of a 'K3' in action, at Stretton Crossing, is tiny and poorly printed, but it is a treasured memento of the days when the dear old beer trains to York and Colwick (see Chapter 4) were often in the hands of these elegant Gresley products. A better effort shows the northbound 'Devonian' at Burton station, with unrebuilt Bristol 'Patriot' No 45504 *Royal Signals* piloted by a 'Black 5'. It brings to mind a fine run from Birmingham behind the 'Pate', and many other such journeys with steam, mainly on the 10.30 Bristol-Newcastle.

Also included here are a few logs from those far-off days; they are approximate, to say the least, and their historical value lies only in their rarity – few people timed trains on that stretch. But to me, and perhaps to other enthusiasts who know the line, they can still communicate a thrill.

In the Winter timetable of 1960-61, the 30-minute schedule of the 10.30 from Bristol made it one of only 19 on the LMR timed at more than 60mph start to stop. However, the timetable planners had failed to note a long 15mph slack for bridge rebuilding at Tamworth, so there was no chance of keeping time until the work was completed, just weeks

Logs: Birmingham New St to Burton-on-Trent										
(1 & 2) 2.15pm Bristol-York.										
(1) 7 September 1963. Loco: 45649. Load: 8.										
(2) 29 April 1961. Loco: 45504. Load: 9.										
(3, 4) 10.30am Bristol-Newcastle.										
(3) 23 September 1961. Loco: 46157. Load: 11.										
(4) 27 May 1961. Loco: 45660. Load: 11.										
(1, 2)	(3, 4)			(1)		(2)		(3, 4)	(3)	(4)	
miles	miles		sched	actual	sched	actual	sched	actual	actual	
0.00	0.00	NEW STREET	0	0.00	0	0.00	0	0.00	0.00	
2.10	2.10	Saltley		3.55		4.15		4.10	4.15	
5.35	5.35	Castle Bromwich		7.00		7.30		7.30	7.40	
7.60	7.60	Water Orton		9.10		9.35		9.35	9.40	
11.80	11.80	Kingsbury		12.55		13.25		13.20	13.10	
15.45	15.45	Wilnecote		16.10		16.55		16.30	16.15	
17.35	17.35	TAMWORTH	20	18.35	20	19.15		18.15	17.45	
4.20	21.55	*Elford*		5.35		6.20		21.30	21.20	
7.60	24.95	*Wichnor Jct*		8.35		9.20		24.30	24.15	
								sigs		
12.85	30.20	BURTON	17	13.30	15	14.40	30	30.00	29.15	
Estimated net times				18½+		19¼+		29½	29¼	
				13½		14¾				
Timings to nearest 5 seconds.										

before the diesels took over in the summer of 1961. My first run after the end of the restriction (No 4 in the log) was also my best ever; appropriately, it was behind 'Jubilee' No 45660 *Rooke*, famous for its record-breaking achievements on the Settle & Carlisle in 1937. To refer once more to *Moved by Steam*, I said there that I'd give a lot for a photograph of the 10.30 at New Street before (dare we say it?) D-Day. Through the kindness of members of the Friends of the National Railway Museum, we're able to include a fine picture of *Rooke*, in the right station, and almost at the right platform.

My earliest Burton pictures date from 1961-59, and they sent me back again to notebooks of those years. How intense a child's feelings are! How much it all meant! Even more vividly than the pictures, these documents preserve the essence of those days, those happy days when the threat of dieselisation was no more than a cloud on the horizon.

The tailpiece to this book is a fragment from the 'Mosaic'; it is another 'Jubilee'; it is at Moor Street Bridge, our favourite haunt in the early spotting years; and it is the down 'Devonian', the express that gave the best chance of the day for a rarity. It was diagrammed for a Leeds Holbeck 'Jubilee' or 'Black 5', but quite often a 'foreigner' was borrowed – Mike (Mick) Thompson, in an unpublished article, conjectured that one particular Holbeck Running Foreman liked to give spotters further south a treat! From time to time over the years such mouth-watering specimens had appeared as *Neptune*, *Valiant*

Above This fine study was taken in 1950 with a Kodak box 'Brownie' camera by George Rutter, en route from Cheltenham Lansdown, where he was a junior booking clerk, to visit his grandfather, the Yardmaster at Bescot. 'Jubilee' No 45660 *Rooke* stands on the through line between platforms 7 and 8 (?) on the Midland Railway side of Birmingham New Street, presumably waiting to take over a northbound service. To the best of the photographer's knowledge this would have been an

unusual occurrence, as trains on the North East-South West route via Birmingham rarely changed engines there. *Rooke*'s condition rivals that of *Barcote Manor* on page 137, and the same phenomenon noted there can be observed in reverse. As the 22A shedplate shows, Barrow Road was still a London Midland depot; after it passed to the Western in early 1958 and became 82E, its locos were still well turned out, but they never had quite this level of TLC. *George Rutter*

Right An extract from Mike's notebook, December 1960. As ever, marks are awarded, imitating the script of much-feared Maths teacher C. F. L. ('Bill') Read. The use of abbreviated names, rather than numbers, for 'namers', and 'c', instead of a tick, for 'cops', follows the practice of Mick Thompson. On the right is our first record of a 'main-line' diesel at Burton, with the query 'is this the start of dieselisation at Burton?' and the later annotation 'How right we were'. *RNI*

Right A year earlier, no diesels, and – what joy! – a Kingmoor 'Jube', on shed after failing with the southbound 'Devonian' the day before. Note the orgy of signatures and Goon names, the stylised 'R' (for 'Right') of another teacher (who?), and the stern injunction that the book 'MUST ONLY BE USED FOR TRAINSPOTTING PURPOSES'. *RNI*

and *Indomitable*, all from Glasgow Corkerhill, or *Swiftsure*, *Ocean* and *Sanspareil* (see above), from Carlisle Kingmoor, and we always hoped for another. The cameo here, violated for the Railway Mosaic and rehabilitated courtesy of Photoshop, is believed to be of a rarity indeed for Burton, but not a Scottish one, and alas a 'wreck' on the Trent Valley line: No 45560 *Prince Edward Island*, then of Liverpool Edge Hill. Whether or not, I can see it now…

ACKNOWLEDGEMENTS

We are delighted that Pete Waterman, known with gratitude and admiration to all railway enthusiasts, has kindly supplied the Foreword. We have included a photograph of Great Western 'Castle' No 5054 *Earl of Ducie* alongside his contribution, as it is the prototype for one of his remarkable collection of models. We are most grateful for his interest in what we have produced.

In *Moved by Steam* we recorded our debt to Mike (or, as we call him here, Mick) Thompson, who not only fostered our interest but also entrusted us with the running of the Club he founded. Sadly Mick died in 2010 and with him a vast body of knowledge of British Railways in the 1950s and '60s.

Again we must acknowledge the help we have received from the many friends who enjoyed *Moved by Steam* and especially for the encyclopaedic information given to us freely by Roger Newman and Cliff Shepherd. Hugh McQuade, of the Severn Valley Railway, has again supplied fascinating facts about coaching stock. A debt of gratitude needs recording as well for the skills of Cambridge University Library Photographic Department in rescuing a film of Mike's after 17 years 'in the can'. The help and advice of Ordnance Survey staff is much appreciated.

No work such as this is free from errors, and any that do remain are, of course, the responsibility of the authors. One disclaimer at least seems called for: the logs were compiled without benefit of a stopwatch.

Peter Townsend, Will Adams and their colleagues at Silver Link Publishing have always been enthusiastic, cheerful, and ready to do their best to fit in with our, often rather definite, ideas! It's been great working with them once again and we are really grateful.

Finally, the Dedication is merely a token acknowledgement of all we owe to the people named in it and pictured on page 6.

ABBREVIATIONS

'BB'	'Battle of Britain'
BR	British Railways
BR(WR)	British Railways (Western Region)
C&HPR	Cromford & High Peak Railway
CKP	Cockermouth, Keswick & Penrith Railway
DDR	Deutsche Demokratische Republik (German Democratic Republic)
DMU	Diesel multiple unit
ECML	East Coast Main Line
EE	English Electric
EWS	English, Welsh & Scottish Railway (now DB Schenker Rail [UK])
GC(R)	Great Central (Railway)
GW(R)	Great Western (Railway)
GN(R)	Great Northern (Railway)
H&S(E)	Health & Safety (Executive)
LMS	London Midland & Scottish
LNE(R)	London & North Eastern (Railway)
LNW(R)	London & North Western (Railway)
LSW(R)	London & South Western (Railway)
MPD	Motive Power Depot
MR	Midland Railway
NSR	North Staffordshire Railway
RCTS	Railway Correspondence & Travel Society
S&C	Settle & Carlisle
S&D(JR)	Somerset & Dorset (Joint Railway)
SR	Southern Railway
WCML	West Coast Main Line
WR	Western Region
WRC	"Wanderers" Railfans' Club
WD	War Department

INDEX OF PHOTOGRAPHIC LOCATIONS

Amlwch 73
Ardrossan MPD 123

Banbury 41
Bala Junction 74-75
Barmouth 70-71, 137
Barnstaple Junction 64
Barton & Walton 87
Basingstoke 25, 37
Bath Green Park 67
Baynards 31
Bedford (near) 6
Bentley Heath 115
Bidston MPD (near) 11
Birkenhead MPD 131
Birmingham New Street 140; Snow Hill 116-117
Blaisdon Halt 50, 52
Blandford Forum 27
Bournemouth Central 133
Branston 86-87
Braunton (near) 4
Brimscombe 51
Bristol Temple Meads 59
Brockenhurst (near) 23
Burton-on-Trent 78-85, 88-90, 98-102, 129, 138, 144
    Allsopp's Maltings branch 88
    Bond End branch 83-84
    Clarence Street 83-84
    Dallow branch 89-91
    Dallow Street 100-101
    Duke Street branch 85
    Horninglow branch 100-101
    Iron Bridges 78-79, 102
    Moor Street 85, 144
    MPD 88, 129
    New Branch 83
    New Street 83, 85
    Station 79-82, 85, 138, 144
    Truman's Brewery 78-79
    Uxbridge Street 83
    Wetmore 99-100
    Woolley's Bridge 98-99

Cambrian Railways 57-58, 68-72, 74-75, 137
Carlisle 20
Carmarthen 134
Cemmes Road 58
Clay Mills 98-99
Corfe Castle 30
Crewe Works 126

Cromford & High Peak Railway 8-9, 11

Dalry Road MPD 124
Darley Dale 10
Dent Head 13
Derby MPD 132; Works 127
Dorchester South 28
Dorking (near) 32; Town 32-34
Dovey Junction 137
Dumfries MPD 122
Dunsbear Halt 62

Eastleigh 38
Egginton Goods 95
Elmhurst Crossing 110
Etwall (near) 95
Evercreech Junction 55, 67
Exeter Central 54; St David's 136

Farnborough 36
Finchdean 31

Garsdale 14
Gloucester Central 51-52
Gunnislake 53

Halwill 62-63
Harlech 72
Hatton (near) 113-114
Haven Street 1
Haymarket MPD 123
Honiton 56

Knowle & Dorridge 114

Lancaster 14, 17
Leamington Spa 112
Lichfield Trent Valley 105-107, 134
Llanymynech 70

Marston Junction 94
Menai Bridge 73-75
Middleton Bottom (near) 11
Monkton & Came Halt 30
Mortehoe & Woolacombe (near) 61
Motherwell MPD 119

Neville Hill MPD 128
Newbury 38
Newport (Pill) MPD 129

Ormskirk 15
Oxenholme (near) 2, 15, 19-20
Oxford 6, 24, 40-47
    Abbey Road 44
    Isis railway bridge 45
    New Hinksey 46-48
    Station 24, 40-43, 48
    Walton Well Road 6

Peak Forest 21-22, back cover
Peterborough North 135
Pilning 68
Potlocks Farm 95
Preston 19

Reading General 39
Redhill MPD 124
Rolleston-on-Dove 93

Salisbury MPD 120
Sandford, front cover
Sandhurst Halt 34
Shap Summit (near) 17

Sidmouth Junction 56
Southampton Central 27
Springs Branch MPD 130
Steeple Grange 8-9
Stenson Junction 96
Stratford MPD 130
Stretton Crossing 92, 138; Junction 90-91
Swindon 39, 134; Works 125

Talerddig (near) 58
Teignmouth 138
Templecombe Lower Platform 66; MPD 66
Tunbridge Wells MPD 125
Tutbury 94

Welshpool 68-69
West Bromwich 7, 117
Whittington 108-109
Willington (Beds) 6; (Derbys) 96-97
Winchester 37
Wiveliscombe 60
Woking 35
Wolverhampton Works 121

The driver of a 'Jubilee' opens up after the observing the 30mph slack round the island platform at Burton with the southbound 'Devonian'. The loco is believed to be No 45560 *Prince Edward Island*, and the date 20 May 1961. *MES*